Baby and Toddler

MEAL PREP PLAN

BATCH COOK A WEEK'S NUTRITIOUS MEALS IN UNDER 2 HOURS

KEDA BLACK

Skyhorse Publishing

CONTENTS

4–6 MONTHS

6–9 MONTHS

9–12 MONTHS

12 MONTHS+

What is batch cooking?

Batch cooking is the idea of cooking in advance for the whole week. In concrete terms, you spend about 2 hours in the kitchen on a Sunday, after doing the shopping, for example. It's about doing the bulk of the work at this time. Then on each weekday, you only need to spend 10 minutes or so in the kitchen to finish preparing and heating your baby's meals.

3

good reasons
to adopt batch cooking

REDUCE STRESS

No more panicking each morning trying to work out what to make for your baby that day. With batch cooking, everything is planned and you don't have to think about it. These little meals from home are also easy to transport and quick to heat up.

EAT BETTER AND ONLY HOMEMADE

Being organised means you have something homemade on hand each day, however simple it is, instead of relying too much on store-bought products.

LESS WASTE

Everything you buy is used. Fresh produce is cooked sooner, especially vegetables, which means they don't clutter up the refrigerator or go mouldy at the bottom of the crisper, and all leftovers are frozen.

HOW TO USE THIS BOOK

1. The weekly meal plan

The list of dishes for the week (lunch, snack and dinner)

The relevant age range for your baby

The time spent in the kitchen on Sunday

The best season for the meal plan

The daily needs of your baby during this stage

Cooking equipment

Storage containers

2. Sunday's results

Photo: everything you will have prepared after your Sunday session in the kitchen

3. Visual shopping guide

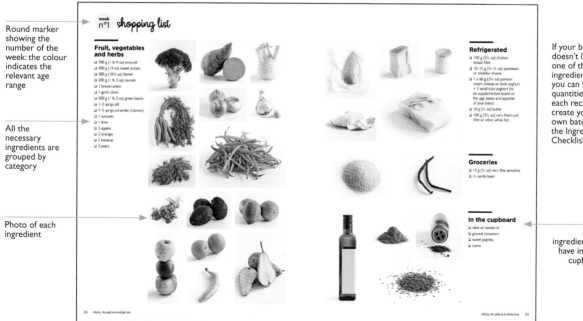

Round marker showing the number of the week: the colour indicates the relevant age range

All the necessary ingredients are grouped by category

Photo of each ingredient

If your baby doesn't like one of the ingredients, you can find quantities for each recipe to create your own batch in the Ingredients Checklist (p.170)

Basic ingredients to have in your cupboard

4. The steps to follow on Sunday

Each step is numbered to help you get organised

The time it takes for each step

Clear pictures illustrating the steps

THE INSTRUCTIONS:

→ BOWL: set the preparation aside in a bowl

→ FREEZER: store the small container in the freezer

The list of containers for the week, day by day

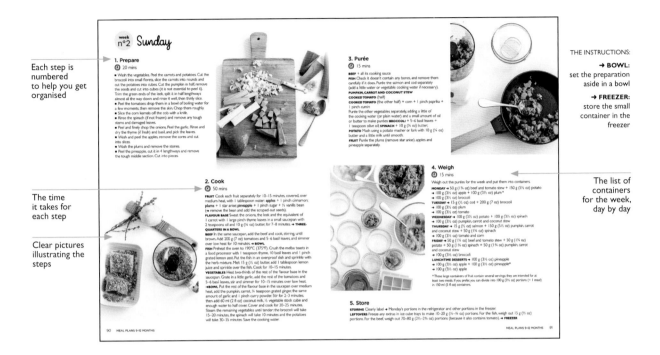

5. For each day of the week

Photos of the finished recipes

The names of the dishes (lunch / snack / dinner)

Preparation time

What preparation is left to do

PRACTICAL ADVICE

NOTICE

This book is not a substitute for official recommendations and for the advice of your doctor, which can change over time and is, above all, specially tailored to each child. It is designed to help you get organised in these specific stages of food diversification.

THE MAIN PERIODS

The meal plans are divided into 4 main periods:
- 4–6 months
- 6–9 months
- 9–12 months
- 12 months+

This division is suggested for the purposes of organisation, simplicity and understanding. It begins with the minimum age for sampling certain foods, which doesn't in any way mean that it is a precise timetable that should be strictly followed. Your child might only start at 6 months, for example, so their meals at 7 months won't be as varied and substantial as those of a child who started earlier. Babies can take their time to taste certain ingredients and textures. The meal plans should be adapted to your baby's own rhythm, tastes, needs, teeth... Often the meal plans allow for a little left over that you can put in the freezer: you can adapt your new meals each week to what you have from the previous week.

COOKING FOR YOUR BABY

Cooking methods

- Steaming, cooking in just a little water in a covered saucepan, and boiling are preferable to other methods, and the first two are better for preserving nutrients. Cook foods for a fairly long time (adjust the cooking times to suit the size of the pieces and the steamer) so that the vegetables are soft and can be puréed easily until smooth. For the very first purées, which are really more about introducing flavours than nutrition, boiling is probably the quickest and most practical option.
- Pan-frying is not suggested for many dishes. When you start preparing small meals (at around 9 months), you can brown food (meat in particular) quickly in a little fat, over medium heat, for the flavour.
- In the beginning, vegetables, fish and meat tend to be cooked separately. This is more practical for combining different foods to suit your baby's tastes and what they are familiar with or have yet to discover, but there's nothing to stop you from breaking free of the meal plans and improvising! Bit by bit, the meals move closer to more traditional ways of cooking, where ingredients are combined for the flavour.

Salt, sugar, fat and spices

Eliminate salt and sugar altogether to start with, and then introduce them sparingly (at about 12 months or a little before, but only very tiny pinches). Fat is not forbidden. Adding a little bit to purées is a quick way of improving their flavour. You can use all kinds of herbs and spices, introducing them little by little in very small quantities, and making sure you purée them well.

Your baby's food can be adapted from the family meal: set aside a portion of pumpkin to cook without salt, purée a small piece of chicken... In the book, the meal plans are designed specifically for babies, which is why some quantities (meat and fish in particular) are very small, but you'll work out how to incorporate them into your overall shopping list.

Equipment

Cooking for your baby doesn't require any special equipment.
- A saucepan and lid
- A steamer, or a Chinese bamboo steamer basket, or a metal steamer insert
- Something for puréeing (blender, processor, stick blender), mashing (masher or fork), or you might even want to use a food mill (it takes longer but it produces a very nice texture). Don't purée potato in a blender or food processor as it will become gluey.
- A kitchen scale to divide up your purées for the week and check quantities of meat or fish (although you will soon be able to judge the amount your baby needs by eye without having to weigh it). As a general rule, 1 teaspoon of meat or fish is equivalent to about 10 g (¼ oz).

Choosing produce

Just as for adults, it's a good idea to eat seasonally. The more organic fruits and vegetables, the better.

Peel fruits and vegetables in the beginning to make very smooth purées. Later, if the fruits and vegetables are organic and well washed, there's no reason to peel everything.

STORAGE

- In theory, a homemade fruit or vegetable purée kept in the refrigerator should be consumed within 48 hours. This is why, when cooking for your baby in advance, we recommend freezing anything that won't be eaten the next day (or the day after). The ideal is to thaw each day's food the day before or in the morning, in the refrigerator of course.
- If you use frozen raw foods, such as peas or spinach, and add them to a dish that is cooked, it is safe to freeze the preparation afterwards.

Quantities

- The quantities suggested in the book are averages. They can be adapted to your own child, although you shouldn't exceed the recommended quantities of protein.
- If you have leftovers, don't hesitate to freeze them in ice cube trays, and once they are frozen you can put the cubes in freezer bags. Don't forget to label your food clearly (weight, date and contents), otherwise you'll quickly lose track.
- When you freeze a preparation, be careful not to fill containers right to the top, especially glass ones: the liquid in the food expands during freezing and can cause the glass to break. Do not refreeze any thawed food.

Containers

You will need 150 ml (5 fl oz) and 250 ml (9 fl oz) jars or containers, and some a little larger for meals for babies who are over 12 months old. You can reuse the jars from store-bought baby foods if you use them. In the meal plans, the foods of the week are stored in small containers, but you can also freeze them in ice cube trays if you don't have enough containers.

DIETARY DIVERSIFICATION

WHAT IS IT?

Diversification is the transitional stage from an exclusively milk-based diet to a varied diet with solids. It can start at around 4 months (never before).

Golden Rule no. 1: Adapt to your baby and move gradually

Listen to your baby and follow the advice of the paediatrician. The diversification schedule is very flexible. If your baby has only started to taste their first fruit and vegetable purées at around 5–6 months, they will not be able to enjoy a near-complete meal at 6 months. The main focus is on your baby developing a good relationship with food, rather than rushing things, and adapting to your baby's rhythm, taste, appetite and teeth.

Golden Rule no. 2: Only one new food at a time

Foods should be introduced one by one, which among other things lets you check whether your baby is allergic to anything. When you start combining foods, make sure there is not more than one unknown food per mixture (including spices and herbs).

UP TO 4 MONTHS

The baby's diet consists only of breast milk or formula.

BETWEEN 4 AND 6 MONTHS

Discovering fruits and vegetables one by one

- **Texture:** very smooth purées
- **Method:** in the beginning, choose one food (for example, a vegetable such as carrot or a fruit such as pear) in the form of a purée and give your baby a spoonful to taste. If your baby wants more, give it to them; if they don't, stop. You can offer it again the next day, then change the fruit/vegetable. If your baby really dislikes the flavour of something, you can either come back to it later or combine it with another fruit or vegetable flavour so they can get used to the taste. There is no rush: milk is still the main food and the vegetables and fruits your baby tastes aren't really about nutritional intake yet.

- **Additions:** nothing in the beginning, then you can add herbs (purée them well with the vegetables) or spices in moderate amounts, and try purées that combine 2 vegetables or 2 fruits.

TOWARDS 6 MONTHS AND UP TO AROUND 9 MONTHS

Introducing meat and fish

- **Texture:** very smooth purées
- **Meal plan:**

Meat or fish: 10–15 g (¼–½ oz) – at lunchtime
Vegetables: 120–300 g (4¼–10½ oz) – as you like, but without forcing it (lunch + optional soup in the evening)
Fruit: gradually increase from 50 g (1¾ oz) to about 130 g (4½ oz)
Milk: 500–900 ml (17–31 fl oz) distributed throughout the day (breakfast, snack, dinner, perhaps lunch), to be replaced in part and very gradually with other dairy products

- **Additions:** introduce a very small teaspoonful of oil or a dab of butter
- **Avoid:** vegetables that are a little hard to digest, such as kale, celery, capsicums (peppers), the green part of leeks

FROM 9–12 MONTHS

More complete meals

- **Texture:** coarser purées
- **Meal plan:**

Meat or fish: 15–20 g (½–¾ oz) – at lunchtime
Vegetables: 200–400 g (7–14 oz) – as you like, but without forcing it (lunch + optional soup in the evening)

Fruit: 2 serves a day, choose between purées (80–100 g/2¾–3½ oz) and thinly sliced fresh fruits
Milk: 500–900 ml (17–31 fl oz) distributed throughout the day, and to be replaced in part and very gradually by other dairy products
Starchy foods: 50 g (1¾ oz) – in the evening (cooked weight)
- **Additions:** offer herbs and spices more often
- **Bonus:** Your baby can sit up in a high chair at the dinner table – diversification also means socialising at meal times!

AFTER 12 MONTHS
Meals almost like those eaten by the grown-ups
- **Texture:** real pieces
- **Meal plan:**
Meat or fish: 20–25 g (¾–1 oz) – at lunchtime, no more than 40 g (1½ oz) up to 2 years of age
Vegetables: 200–500 g (7 oz–1 lb 2 oz) – as you like, but without forcing it (lunch + optional soup in the evening)
Fruit: 3–4 serves a day, alternating fresh fruits and purées
Milk: About 500 ml (17 fl oz) + 1 other dairy product spread throughout the day. Partly and gradually replace milk with other dairy products
Starchy foods: 75–100 g (2½–3½ oz) – in the evening (cooked weight)
- **Additions:** herbs, spices, oil/butter in reasonable quantities
- **Bonus:** your baby can sample a lightly sweetened cake for their birthday, and discover the pleasure of chocolate

NO-NOS AND PRECAUTIONS...

Potentially allergenic foods: recommendations vary. Some doctors advise giving them early on, in very small quantities, to limit the risk of future allergy, while others continue to recommend caution (e.g. strawberries from 8 months, kiwifruit from 12 months).

Honey: not before 12 months (or in very small quantities added during cooking, for example) – risk of bacteria.

Raw milk cheeses: may contain potentially harmful bacteria that the baby's body is less able to resist than an adult's.

Nuts (hazelnuts, almonds, walnuts, etc.): allergy risk, and choking risk when offered whole.

Shellfish and crustaceans: allergy risk.

Salt and sugar: eliminate from the daily diet. Fruits and vegetables already contain enough sugar, and herbs, spices or other aromatics can play the role of flavour enhancers. Even so, it's okay for your baby to try a lightly sweetened cake or biscuit from time to time, and they are entitled to exceptions on special occasions like everyone else.

Lentils and other legumes: these are very good foods, in particular because they are good sources of protein. Since they can sometimes be a bit difficult to digest, they are more usually recommended from 9 months (or 12 months) on, in small quantities.

Pork: generally not recommended before 12 months, unless it is very lean. Overall, meats that are too fatty are to be avoided, even though, once again, we shouldn't be afraid of a moderate amount of fat in the diet, which will gradually replace the fats contained in breast milk or formula, and are essential for the body to function. In any case, cook meats for babies and young children very well.

Egg: usually not recommended earlier than 9 months or even 12 months, especially egg white, which is considered to be allergenic. It also depends on the family, and whether there is any inherited predisposition to allergies or not. In any case, eggs are high in fat and protein, so start your baby with a quarter of an egg, then a half, before tackling a whole one (after 12 months), well cooked for now!

SEASONAL PRODUCE

Autumn

Vegetables

Beetroot
Broccoli (end of season)
Cabbage
Carrots
Celery and celeriac
Corn
Fennel (end of season)
Garlic
Leeks
Onions
Parsnips
Potatoes
Pumpkin
Silverbeet (more in spring, but sometimes
  available in autumn)
Spinach (end of season)
Tomatoes (some tomatoes until April)
Turnips
Winter salad leaves

Fruit

Apples
Blueberries
Chestnuts
Figs (in April)
Grapes
Kiwifruit
Lemons
Mandarins
Oranges (end of season)
Pears
Quince
Raspberries (until April)

Winter

Vegetables

Beetroot
Cabbage
Carrots
Celery and celeriac
Corn
Garlic
Leeks
Onions
Parsnips
Potatoes
Pumpkin
Silverbeet (more in spring, but sometimes
  available in winter)
Turnips
Winter salad leaves

You can use frozen peas and green beans,
and good-quality tinned tomatoes for sauces.

Fruit

Apples
Clementines
Grapefruit
Kiwifruit
Lemons
Mandarins
Oranges
Pears

IT'S THE SEASON!

In any season, give local food networks first preference
over the supermarket: community-supported agriculture,
farmers' markets and stores that sell local products.
Vegetables in season have more flavour, even if things can
get a bit monotonous by the end of winter. You can cheer
up winter with frozen foods, but choose good-quality ones,
such as frozen peas or broad beans, or frozen raspberries.

FROM SEPTEMBER TO MARCH...

This is really the time when vegetables are easy to use
and don't need much preparation. There's no need to peel
organic vegetables: if their skin is very thin, a simple brush or
even rinse will do. If you have too many herbs or other leafy
vegetables (watercress, for example), you can also freeze
them for later to use in soups or purées for your baby.

Spring

Vegetables

Artichokes
Asparagus
Baby beetroot
Baby leeks
Baby turnips
Broad beans
Broccoli
Bulb spring onions (scallions)
Carrots
Cauliflower
Celery
Cucumbers
Fennel
Green beans, flat beans, shelling beans
Peas
Potatoes
Radishes
Silverbeet
Spinach
Spring lettuces
Zucchini (courgettes)

Fruit

Apricots (in December)
Blackcurrants (in December)
Cherries (in December)
Grapefruit
Redcurrants (in December)
Rhubarb
Strawberries
Watermelon

Summer

Vegetables

Artichokes
Broccoli
Bulb spring onions
Capsicums (peppers)
Celery
Cucumbers
Eggplant (aubergine)
Green bean, flat beans, shelling beans
Potatoes
Radishes
Silverbeet
Spinach
Spring carrots
Summer lettuces
Tomatoes
Zucchini (courgettes)

Fruit

Apricots
Blackberries
Blackcurrants
Blueberries
Figs (at the end of summer)
Grapes (at the end of summer)
Mangoes
Melons
Nectarines
Peaches
Plums
Raspberries
Redcurrants
Strawberries
Watermelon

Meal plans 4-6 months

basic recipes

Vegetable purées

Carrot

Broccoli

Cauliflower

Zucchini

Green bean

Pea

Sweet potato

Potato

Pumpkin

Corn

Avocado

Parsnip

Fruit purées

Apple

Pear

Peach

Apricot

Plum

Mango

Banana

Raspberry

Season:

Choose fruits and vegetables in season.

Daily requirements

A spoonful of very smooth fruit and/or vegetable purée, without forcing it, as much as your child wants.

Mainly milk-based diet.

For storing

Ice cube trays

Equipment

1 steamer

1 saucepan

1 blender or food processor for puréeing

Vegetable purées

Carrot purée

 5–20 mins

❏ 500 g (1 lb 2 oz) carrots

Peel and wash the carrots, remove the ends, and slice into rounds. Place the rounds in a saucepan, cover with water and bring to the boil, then lower the heat a little and simmer gently for about 15 minutes or until tender. Purée in a blender or food processor until very smooth, adding a little of the cooking water if needed.

A LITTLE EXTRA Add a pinch of cinnamon, cumin, or a few fresh coriander (cilantro) leaves (add to the cooking water from the beginning).

Broccoli purée

 10–15 mins

❏ 600 g (1 lb 5 oz) broccoli

Remove the tough parts of the stem (you can peel them and keep the core, which is very tender) and separate the head into florets. Place them in a steamer basket over some water in a saucepan. Cover and cook for about 10 minutes. Purée in a blender or food processor.

A LITTLE EXTRA Add a little cottage cheese when puréeing the broccoli.

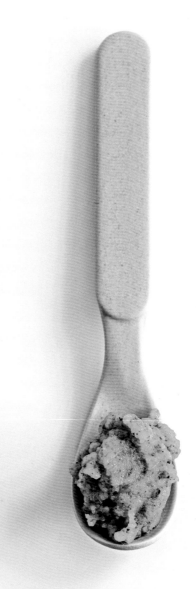

Cauliflower purée

 10–15 mins

❏ 600 g (1 lb 5 oz) cauliflower

Separate the cauliflower into florets. Place in a steamer basket or a saucepan of water. Cover and cook for about 10 minutes. Purée in a blender or food processor.

A LITTLE EXTRA Gently simmer the cauliflower in 300 ml (10½ fl oz) milk and/or add just a little bit of butter: these dairy products (in small quantities here) soften the flavour.

Zucchini purée

 10–15 mins

❏ 500 g (1 lb 2 oz) zucchini (courgettes)

Wash and peel the zucchini. If the skin is thin, don't remove it completely (it will add flavour and texture). Slice into rounds and steam (or simmer in a saucepan in just enough water to cover) for 10 minutes. Purée in a blender or food processor with enough cooking water to make a smooth purée.

Vegetable purées

Green bean purée

 10–15 mins

❑ 600 g (1 lb 5 oz) green beans, strings removed

Trim the beans. Cook in a saucepan of boiling water for about 10 minutes, depending on the size of the beans. Drain and purée in a blender or food processor.

A LITTLE EXTRA Add a few basil leaves.

Pea purée

 10–15 mins

❑ 500 g (1 lb 2 oz) shelled peas (1.5 kg/3 lb 5 oz unshelled weight)

Place the peas in a saucepan with 250 ml (17 fl oz) water. Cook over medium heat for about 10 minutes. Purée until very smooth in a blender or food processor. The little skins can be removed by putting the purée through a fine strainer (or you can have your baby get used to them).

A LITTLE EXTRA Add 1 tablespoon thick yoghurt and/or 3–4 mint leaves.

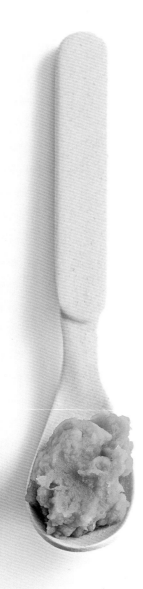

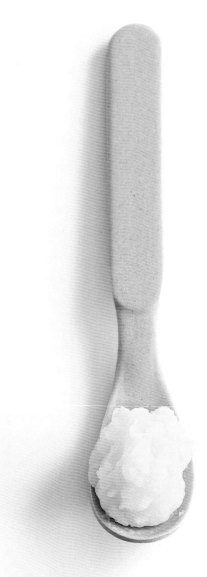

Sweet potato purée

🕐 20–25 mins

❑ 500 g (1 lb 2 oz) sweet potato

Peel the sweet potato, rinse and cut into cubes. Cover with cold water in a saucepan. Bring to the boil, lower the heat a little and cook for about 20 minutes (depending on the size of the cubes – they need to be very tender). Purée in a blender or food processor or mash with a potato masher.

A LITTLE EXTRA Purée with a few leaves of flat-leaf parsley, a sprig of chervil or a tiny pinch of sweet paprika. You can also add a little butter.

Mashed potato

🕐 20–25 mins

❑ 500 g (1 lb 2 oz) mashing potatoes

Peel the potatoes, rinse and cut into cubes. Cover with cold water in a saucepan. Bring to the boil, lower the heat a little and cook for about 20 minutes (depending on the size of the cubes – they need to be very tender). Mash with a potato masher. Avoid using a blender or food processor, as this tends to give them a gluey consistency.

A LITTLE EXTRA Grate a hint of nutmeg into the mashed potato. You can also add 10 g (¼ oz) butter and 100 ml (3½ fl oz) milk.

Vegetable purées

Pumpkin purée

🕐 15–25 mins

❑ 500 g (1 lb 2 oz) butternut or other pumpkin

Peel the pumpkin, remove the seeds and cut into cubes.
Place in a saucepan and cover with water. Bring to the
boil, lower the heat a little and simmer gently for about
15–20 minutes. Purée.

A LITTLE EXTRA Add a few flat-leaf parsley leaves.

Corn purée

🕐 15–25 mins

❑ 2 corn cobs (avoid using tinned corn, which usually
   contains added salt and sugar)

Cook the corn cobs in a saucepan of boiling water for
about 15–20 minutes. Slice the kernels off the cob using
a knife and purée in a blender or food processor. If your
baby doesn't like the texture with the little kernel skins,
pass the purée through a fine strainer.

A LITTLE EXTRA Add coriander (cilantro) leaves, sweet
paprika or a little cottage cheese, or combine the corn
purée with potatoes, carrots or broccoli.

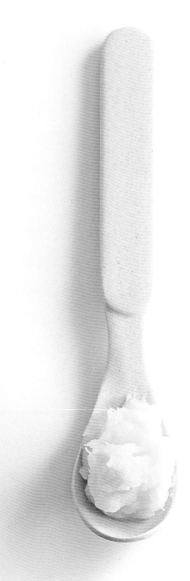

Avocado purée

 5 mins

❏ I ripe avocado

❏ a few drops of lemon juice

Cut the avocado in half and remove the stone. Scoop out the flesh with a spoon and purée in a blender or food processor with a few drops of lemon juice (which prevents it from browning).

A LITTLE EXTRA Add some coriander (cilantro) leaves or sweet paprika.

Parsnip purée

 15–20 mins

❏ 500 g (1 lb 2 oz) parsnips

Peel and wash the parsnips, trim the ends, then slice into rounds. Place them in a saucepan and cover with water. Bring to the boil, lower the heat a little and simmer gently for about 15 minutes or until tender. Purée in a blender or food processor until very smooth, adding a little of the cooking water if needed.

A LITTLE EXTRA Add 2 apple quarters to the parsnip rounds when cooking to sweeten the flavour, and/or some cream when puréeing.

Fruit purées

Apple purée

🕐 15–20 mins

❏ 500 g (1 lb 2 oz) apples (about 5 apples)

Wash and peel the apples. Remove the core and slice or cut into cubes. Place them in a saucepan, half cover with water and cook over medium heat for about 15 minutes. Purée.

A LITTLE EXTRA Add a pinch of cinnamon, a clove (remove before puréeing), ½ vanilla bean (split in half, with the seeds scraped out at the end of cooking). You can also combine the apple with some banana (cook them together).

Pear purée

🕐 15–20 mins

❏ 500 g (1 lb 2 oz) pears (about 5 pears)

Wash and peel the pears. Remove the core and slice or cut into cubes. Place them in a saucepan, half cover with water and cook over medium heat for about 15 minutes. Purée.

A LITTLE EXTRA Add the seeds of a vanilla bean, as for the apples.

Peach purée

🕐 10–15 mins

❑ 500 g (1 lb 2 oz) peaches (about 5 peaches)

Wash and peel the peaches, cut them in half and remove the stone, then slice. Place them in a saucepan, half cover with water and cook over medium heat for about 10 minutes. Purée.

A LITTLE EXTRA Add a strip of lemon rind removed with a vegetable peeler, the seeds of a vanilla bean or a star anise.

Apricot purée

🕐 20–25 mins

❑ 500 g (1 lb 2 oz) apricots

Wash the apricots, cut them in half, remove the stone and cut them into quarters. Place them in a saucepan, half cover with water and cook over medium heat for about 10 minutes. Purée.

A LITTLE EXTRA Add the seeds of a vanilla bean. You can also make a purée from dried apricots, adding water to almost cover and cooking for about 20 minutes until they are very tender. You can add spices to the cooking liquid (star anise, cinnamon stick, clove) and remove them before puréeing.

Fruit purées

Plum purée

🕐 10–15 mins

 500 g (1 lb 2 oz) plums

Wash the plums, cut in half, remove the stone, place in a saucepan and half cover with water. Cook over medium heat for about 10 minutes before puréeing.

A LITTLE EXTRA Cinnamon and vanilla go well with plums.

Mango purée

🕐 5 mins

 1 ripe mango

Wash the mango and slice down either side of the stone to remove the 'cheeks'. Score the flesh of the cheeks in a crisscross pattern, without cutting through the skin, and then cut along the inside to remove the cubes. Purée.

Banana purée

 10–15 mins

❑ 4 bananas

Peel the bananas and slice them into rounds. Place them in a saucepan, half cover with water and cook over medium heat for about 10 minutes. Purée or mash.

A LITTLE EXTRA Add a little cinnamon, 1 star anise or 2–3 cardamom pods and remove them before puréeing.

Raspberry purée

 10 mins

❑ 500 g (1 lb 2 oz) raspberries (fresh or frozen)

Place the raspberries in a saucepan with 1 tablespoon of water (this isn't necessary if they are frozen, as they will give off more liquid) and simmer very gently for 7–8 minutes. Purée. If you'd rather remove the small seeds, pass through a strainer or a fine food mill.

Meal plans 6–9 months

sample week n°1

Timing

1 HR 30 MIN IN THE KITCHEN

Season: spring

In other seasons, replace the broccoli with zucchini (courgette), the green beans with peas, and the fennel with celeriac.

Daily requirements*

Meat or fish:
10–15 g (¼–½ oz) at lunchtime

Vegetables: 120–300 g
(4¼–10½ oz)

Fruit: build up gradually
from 50 g (1¾ oz) to
130 g (4½ oz)

Milk and dairy products:
500–900 ml (17–31 fl oz)

*Check the recommendations
of your paediatrician.

Monday

Orange chicken, fennel and carrot
Apple purée and cream cheese
Broccoli soup

Tuesday

Cod, sweet potato and broccoli
Mashed banana and cinnamon
Carrot purée

Wednesday

Orange chicken and green beans
Pear purée
Broccoli and sweet potato soup

Thursday

Cod and dill broccoli
Apple and pear purée
Green bean purée

Friday

Semolina with cheese
and carrot purée
Mashed banana
Fennel and sweet potato purée

bonus recipe

Creamy guacamole

For storing

9 x 150 ml (5 fl oz)
containers
4 x 250 ml (9 fl oz)
containers
4 ice cube trays

Equipment

1 steamer
1 large saucepan
1 blender or food
processor for puréeing

shopping list

Fruit, vegetables and herbs

- ❏ 700 g (1 lb 9 oz) broccoli
- ❏ 400 g (14 oz) sweet potato
- ❏ 300 g (10½ oz) fennel
- ❏ 500 g (1 lb 2 oz) carrots
- ❏ 1 brown onion
- ❏ 1 garlic clove
- ❏ 500 g (1 lb 2 oz) green beans
- ❏ 1–2 sprigs dill
- ❏ 4–5 sprigs coriander (cilantro)
- ❏ 1 avocado
- ❏ 1 lime
- ❏ 3 apples
- ❏ 2 oranges
- ❏ 2 bananas
- ❏ 3 pears

Refrigerated

- ☐ 100 g (3½ oz) chicken breast fillet
- ☐ 10–15 g (¼–½ oz) parmesan or cheddar cheese
- ☐ 1 x 60 g (2¼ oz) portion cream cheese or thick yoghurt + 2 small tubs yoghurt (to be supplemented based on the age, tastes and appetite of your baby)
- ☐ 10 g (¼ oz) butter
- ☐ 100 g (3½ oz) very fresh cod fillet or other white fish

Groceries

- ☐ 15 g (½ oz) very fine semolina
- ☐ ½ vanilla bean

In the cupboard

- ☐ olive or canola oil
- ☐ ground cinnamon
- ☐ sweet paprika
- ☐ cumin

Sunday

1. Prepare

🕐 20 mins

- Wash the vegetables. Peel the carrots and sweet potato. Cut the broccoli into small florets, slice the carrots into rounds, the sweet potato into cubes, and thinly slice the fennel. Trim the green beans, making sure you remove any strings.
- Peel and finely chop the onion and garlic (you will need some onion for the chicken, some garlic for the fish, and a mixture of the two for the vegetables).
- Rinse and dry the dill and coriander, and pick the leaves (save 2 coriander sprigs for the guacamole).
- Wash and peel the apples and pears, remove the cores and cut into slices.

2. Cook

🕐 40 mins

FRUITS Cook the following separately for 10–15 minutes, covered, over medium heat, with 1 tablespoon water: the pears + 1 pinch cinnamon; the apples + vanilla (split ½ vanilla bean in two and scrape the seeds into the apples).

VEGETABLES Steam the vegetables (they can be cooked together, but don't mix them up so you can remove them separately) or boil them, with a little of the chopped garlic and onion: 30–35 minutes for the sweet potato and carrots, about 15–20 minutes for the broccoli, green beans and fennel (adjust the cooking time if needed – the vegetables should be tender). Reserve the cooking water.

PROTEIN Steam the chicken with a little onion for 30–35 minutes. It needs to be well cooked.

Steam the fish with a little garlic for 10–15 minutes.

3. Purée until smooth

 15 mins

CHICKEN with a little of the cooked onion + ½ teaspoon olive oil + 2 teaspoons orange juice + some cooking water from the vegetables if needed for puréeing (or plain water)

FISH Check that it doesn't contain any bones, and remove them carefully if it does. Purée the cod (with the garlic) with a few drops of olive oil.

VEGETABLES Purée the cooked vegetables separately (with the garlic and onion that was cooked with them), adding a little of the cooking water (or plain water if there is none left). Set aside in bowls as you go:

FENNEL + a little olive oil

CARROT + 10–12 coriander leaves + ½ teaspoon olive oil

HALF OF THE BROCCOLI + a few drops olive oil

OTHER HALF OF THE BROCCOLI + dill + a tiny bit of butter

SWEET POTATO + a little butter +1 pinch paprika and cumin

GREEN BEANS + a little olive oil

FRUITS Purée the apples and pears separately.

4. Weigh

 15 mins

Weigh out the purées for the week and put them into containers.

MONDAY → 10 g (¼ oz) orange chicken + 100 g (3½ oz) fennel + 100 g (3½ oz) carrot
→ 100 g (3½ oz) apple
→ 100 g (3½ oz) plain broccoli

TUESDAY → 10 g (¼ oz) cod + 100 g (3½ oz) sweet potato + 100 g (3½ oz) plain broccoli
→ 100 g (3½ oz) carrot

WEDNESDAY → 10 g (¼ oz) orange chicken + 200 g (7 oz) green beans
→ 100 g (3½ oz) pear
→ 50 g (1¾ oz) dill broccoli + 50 g (1¾ oz) sweet potato

THURSDAY → 10 g (¼ oz) cod + 200 g (7 oz) dill broccoli
→ 50 g (1¾ oz) apple + 50 g (1¾ oz) pear
→ 100 g (3½ oz) green beans

FRIDAY → 100 g (3½ oz) carrot
→ 50 g (1¾ oz) sweet potato + 50 g (1¾ oz) fennel

5. Store

STORING Clearly label → Monday's portions in the refrigerator and other portions in the freezer.

LEFTOVERS Freeze any extras in ice cube trays, which will make 10–20 g (¼–¾ oz) portions to use later, combined however you like. For the puréed fish and chicken, weigh out 10 g (¼ oz) portions.

TIP You can use larger containers for the fruit purées, but they must be consumed within 48 hours after thawing.
    If your baby isn't eating vegetables in the evening yet, you can still make the dinner portions and freeze them for later in 100 g (3½ oz) portions in containers or ice cube trays.

Monday

Orange chicken, fennel and carrot /
Apple purée and cream cheese / Broccoli soup

🕐 Ready in 10 mins

LUNCH Reheat the orange chicken, fennel and carrot purées.
SNACK Serve some apple purée with some cream cheese or thick yoghurt.
DINNER Reheat the plain broccoli purée and add some water to make a soup-like consistency.

Cod, sweet potato and broccoli /
Mashed banana and cinnamon / Carrot purée

🕐 Ready in 10 mins

LUNCH Reheat the cod, sweet potato and broccoli purées. You can offer them separately
or make a little mixture (the sweet potato softens the flavour of the broccoli).
SNACK Mash ½ ripe banana in a little yoghurt and sprinkle with cinnamon.
DINNER Reheat the carrot purée.

Wednesday

Orange chicken and green beans /
Pear purée / Broccoli and sweet potato soup

🕐 Ready in 10 mins

LUNCH Reheat the orange chicken and green bean purées.
SNACK Serve some pear purée. If you have whole, ripe pears, you can also purée one at snack time so your baby can taste the fruit raw.
DINNER Gently reheat the broccoli and sweet potato purées and add some water to make a soup-like consistency.

Cod and dill broccoli / Apple and pear purée / Green bean purée

🕐 Ready in 10 mins

LUNCH Reheat the cod and dill broccoli purées.
SNACK Serve a yoghurt with some apple and pear purée.
DINNER Reheat a 100 g (3½ oz) container of green beans. If your baby didn't like the beans the day before, you can also choose something from what is frozen in the ice cube trays (carrot, for example).

Semolina with cheese and carrot purée / Mashed banana / Fennel and sweet potato purée

🕐 Ready in 10 mins

LUNCH Make the semolina with cheese: finely grate the cheese. Heat 150 ml (5 fl oz) water in a saucepan, pour in the semolina, stir and cook for 2–3 minutes to make a porridge. Add 1–2 teaspoons cheese. Reheat the carrot purée to serve alongside.

SNACK Mash some banana, adding a dash of orange juice if you like.

DINNER Reheat the fennel and sweet potato purées.

Creamy guacamole

🕐 Ready in 10 mins

Peel the avocado (it must be completely ripe), purée with a dash of lime and a few coriander leaves, and add a pinch of cumin and sweet paprika. Mix with 60 g (2¼ oz) cream cheese or thick yoghurt. Offer this as an extra with a meal or even as a snack. A whole avocado will make much too much for a baby: the whole family can enjoy it!

Meal plans 6-9 months

sample week n°2

Timing

1 HR 30 MIN
IN THE KITCHEN

Season: winter

In other seasons, replace the celeriac with pumpkin.

Daily requirements*

Meat or fish: 10–15 g (¼–½ oz) at lunchtime

Vegetables: 120–300 g (4¼–10½ oz)

Fruit: build up gradually from 50 g (1¾ oz) to 130 g (4½ oz)

Milk and dairy products: 500–900 ml (17–31 fl oz)

*Check the recommendations of your paediatrician.

Monday

Turkey and chestnuts with celeriac and potatoes
Mango smoothie
Cauliflower and spinach soup

Tuesday

Herbed salmon with cauliflower and spinach purée
Cream cheese and mango coulis
Carrot and corn soup

Wednesday

Polenta and cheese with spinach purée
Apple and mango purée
Celeriac and apple soup

Thursday

Turkey and corn with carrot purée
Mashed banana with yoghurt
Carrot and cauliflower soup

Friday

Herbed salmon with spinach, corn and potato
Apple purée and yoghurt
Cauliflower purée with cheese

bonus recipe

Steamed banana with orange juice

For storing

9 x 150 ml (5 fl oz) containers

4 x 250 ml (9 fl oz) containers

4 ice cube trays

Equipment

1 steamer

1 cast-iron pot or saucepan

1 deep frying pan or saucepan

1 blender or food processor for puréeing

week n°2 shopping list

Fruit, vegetables and herbs

- ❏ 500 g (1 lb 2 oz) cauliflower
- ❏ 500 g (1 lb 2 oz) potatoes
- ❏ 500 g (1 lb 2 oz) carrots
- ❏ 1 small celeriac, about 500 g (1 lb 2 oz)
- ❏ 1 kg (2 lb 4 oz) fresh spinach or about 300 g (10½ oz) frozen
- ❏ a few chives
- ❏ ½ bunch flat-leaf parsley
- ❏ 400 g (14 oz) corn cobs (about 2 cobs) or 200 g (7 oz) kernels (no added salt or sugar)
- ❏ 100 g (3½ oz) plain cooked chestnuts (vacuum-packed or in jars)
- ❏ 1 French shallot
- ❏ a small piece fresh ginger
- ❏ 5 apples
- ❏ 1 orange
- ❏ 3 bananas
- ❏ 300 g (10½ oz) frozen mango or 1 large ripe mango

Refrigerated

- ❏ 100 g (3½ oz) turkey breast
- ❏ 20–30 g (¾–1 oz) parmesan cheese
- ❏ 250 ml (9 fl oz) milk
- ❏ 25 g (1 oz) butter
- ❏ 60 g (2¼ oz) portion cream cheese or thick yoghurt + 2 small tubs yoghurt (to be supplemented according to your baby's needs)
- ❏ 100 g (3½ oz) salmon fillet

Groceries

- ❏ 2 star anise
- ❏ 40 g (1½ oz) polenta
- ❏ 1 organic salt-free vegetable stock cube

In the cupboard

- ❏ olive oil
- ❏ sweet paprika
- ❏ nutmeg
- ❏ sugar

week n°2 Sunday

1. Prepare

🕐 20 mins

- Wash and peel the vegetables. Slice the carrots into rounds, cut the celeriac and potatoes into cubes, separate the cauliflower into florets. Rinse and pick over the spinach if using fresh.
- Slice the kernels off the cob.
- Peel and chop the French shallot.
- Rinse, dry and pick off the parsley leaves. Wash and dry the chives.
- Cut the turkey into pieces.
- Wash the mango and slice along the stone to get two 'cheeks'. Score the flesh inside each cheek in a criss-cross pattern without cutting through the skin, then run the knife along the skin to remove the cubes of flesh.
- Wash and peel the apples, remove the cores and cut into slices.

2. Cook

🕐 40 mins

APPLES Cook the apple, covered, with 1 tablespoon water and a star anise over fairly low heat for 15–20 minutes.

VEGETABLES Steam the carrots and celeriac for about 25 minutes, and the cauliflower for 20 minutes, crumbling a little of the stock cube into the water. Save the cooking water. Boil the potatoes for about 20 minutes. Melt 10 g (¼ oz) butter in a saucepan or deep frying pan, add the spinach and cook with 100 ml (3½ fl oz) water for 7–8 minutes (the fresh spinach will cook in this time – it will reduce down a lot – and the frozen spinach will thaw).

TURKEY In a saucepan or cast-iron pot, sweat the shallot for 6–7 minutes in 2 teaspoons olive oil. Stir in ¼ teaspoon finely grated ginger, add the turkey and stir for 2–3 minutes. Add enough water (use the vegetable cooking water) to half cover the turkey, cover with a lid and simmer for 20 minutes over fairly low heat. Add some of the parsley leaves.

SALMON Heat some of the left-over cooking water (or some water with a few crumbs of stock cube) in a saucepan, enough to cover the salmon. When it comes to a simmer, add the salmon. Cook for about 5 minutes, cover and allow to cool.

3. Purée until smooth

 15 mins

SALMON + half the parsley + the chives

TURKEY Purée half the turkey and shallot mixture + half the corn kernels + some cooking water to obtain a fairly smooth purée. Purée the other half of the turkey and shallot mixture + chestnuts.

VEGETABLES Purée the vegetables separately, adding a little cooking water (as much as you need to obtain a smooth consistency) and a small quantity of fat, setting them aside in bowls as you go:

REST OF THE CORN + 1 pinch sweet paprika + 1 teaspoon butter

SPINACH + 1 pinch sugar (more to season than sweeten)

CARROTS + a little flat-leaf parsley + 1 teaspoon olive oil

CAULIFLOWER + a little nutmeg and milk (use instead of the cooking water to thin out the purée)

CELERIAC + 1 teaspoon olive oil

POTATO Mash it with 10 g (¼ oz) butter + a little milk (don't purée it in a blender or food processor – it will become sticky and gluey).

FRUIT Purée the apples (remove the star anise) and raw mango separately.

4. Weigh

 15 mins

Weigh out the purées for the week and put them into containers.

MONDAY ➜ 30–40 g (1–1½ oz) turkey with chestnuts + 100 g (3½ oz) celeriac + 100 g (3½ oz) potatoes
➜ 100 g (3½ oz) mango
➜ 80 g (2¾ oz) cauliflower + 20 g (¾ oz) spinach

TUESDAY ➜ 10–15 g (¼–½ oz) salmon + 150 g (5½ oz) cauliflower + 50 g (1¾ oz) spinach
➜ 100 g (3½ oz) mango
➜ 70 g (2½ oz) carrot + 30 g (1 oz) corn

WEDNESDAY ➜ 100 g (3½ oz) spinach
➜ 50 g (1¾ oz) apple + 50 g (1¾ oz) mango
➜ 80 g (2¾ oz) celeriac + 20 g (¾ oz) apple

THURSDAY ➜ 30–40 g (1–1½ oz) turkey and corn + 180 g (6 oz) carrot
➜ 50 g (1¾ oz) carrot + 50 g (1¾ oz) cauliflower

FRIDAY ➜ 10–15 g (¼–½ oz) salmon + 100 g (3½ oz) spinach + 50 g (1¾ oz) potato + 50 g (1¾ oz) corn
➜ 100 g (3½ oz) apple
➜ 100 g (3½ oz) cauliflower + 10 g (¼ oz) grated parmesan

5. Store

STORING Clearly label ➜ Monday's portions in the refrigerator and other portions in the freezer.

IMPORTANT: Don't freeze anything that contains thawed mango.

LEFTOVERS Freeze any extras in ice cube trays, which will make 10–20 g (¼–¾ oz) portions to use later, combined however you like. For the puréed fish, weigh out 10–15 g (¼–½ oz) portions. For the turkey, weigh out 30–40 g (1–1½ oz) portions (since it is mixed with chestnuts or corn).

Monday

Turkey and chestnuts with celeriac and potatoes / Mango smoothie / Cauliflower and spinach soup

🕐 Ready in 10 mins

LUNCH Reheat the turkey and chestnuts, celeriac and potato purées.
SNACK Whisk the portion of mango purée with yoghurt. Add milk to give the smoothie the consistency of a drinking yoghurt (you can also use formula).
DINNER Reheat the cauliflower and spinach purées and add some water to make a soup-like consistency.

Herbed salmon with cauliflower and spinach purée
Cream cheese and mango coulis / Carrot and corn soup

⏱ Ready in 10 mins

LUNCH Reheat the salmon, cauliflower and spinach purées.
SNACK Use the portion of mango purée to flavour a cream cheese portion or thick yoghurt.
DINNER Reheat the carrot and corn purées and add some water to make a soup-like consistency.

Wednesday

Polenta and cheese with spinach purée /
Apple and mango purée / Celeriac and apple soup

🕐 Ready in 10 mins

LUNCH Reheat the spinach purée. For the polenta, heat 90 ml (3 fl oz) milk. Take it off the heat, add 10 g (¼ oz) grated parmesan cheese and the polenta in a stream, stirring constantly. Keep stirring after you take it off the heat (the mixture will thicken). Make sure you don't serve it too hot! Serve with the spinach purée on top or separately.

SNACK Serve the apple and mango purée. Supplement with a bottle of milk or a dairy product if needed.

DINNER Reheat the celeriac and apple purées and add some water to make a soup-like consistency.

Turkey and corn with carrot purée /
Mashed banana with yoghurt / Carrot and cauliflower soup

🕐 Ready in 10 mins

LUNCH Reheat the turkey, corn and carrot purées.
SNACK Mash a banana and mix it with a little yoghurt.
DINNER Reheat the carrot and cauliflower purées, which can be thinned out with a little milk to make a soup.

Herbed salmon with spinach, corn and potato / Apple purée and yoghurt / Cauliflower purée with cheese

⏱ Ready in 10 mins

LUNCH Reheat the salmon, spinach, corn and potato purées.
SNACK Serve the apple purée, adding some yoghurt.
DINNER Reheat the cauliflower purée with cheese and add some water to make a soup-like consistency.

Steamed banana with orange juice

🕐 Ready in 15 mins

Steam an unpeeled banana for 10 minutes, or bake in the oven for 10–15 minutes at 180°C (350°F). Meanwhile, squeeze an orange and heat the juice with a star anise. Once the banana is cooked, open it up and drizzle with the juice. Let it cool to lukewarm and serve with a teaspoon. You can add a little yoghurt to the banana pulp.

Meal plans 6–9 months

sample week n°3

Timing

1 HR 30 MIN
IN THE KITCHEN

Season: summer

In other seasons, use tinned peeled tomatoes, frozen raspberries instead of strawberries, and replace the peaches and apricots with apples and pears.

Daily requirements*

Meat or fish: 10–15 g (¼–½ oz) at lunchtime

Vegetables: 120–300 g (4¼–10½ oz)

Fruit: build up gradually from 50 g (1¾ oz) to 130 g (4½ oz)

Milk and dairy products: 500–900 ml (17–31 fl oz)

*Check the recommendations of your paediatrician.

Monday
Ratatouille and sea bream
Peach purée
Broad and green bean soup with mint

Tuesday
Veal and green vegetables
Yoghurt and strawberry purée
Gazpacho

Wednesday
Semolina and tomato
Peach and apricot purée
Zucchini and basil purée

Thursday
Sea bream, mashed potato and tomato purée
Strawberry smoothie
Green bean purée

Friday
Veal and ratatouille
Strawberry and apricot purée
Tomato soup

bonus recipe
Baba ghanoush

For storing

12 x 150 ml (5 fl oz) containers

4 x 250 ml (9 fl oz) containers

4 ice cube trays

Equipment

1 steamer

1 cast-iron pot or saucepan

1 blender or food processor for puréeing

shopping list

Fruit, vegetables and herbs

- ❏ 700 g (1 lb 9 oz) tomatoes
- ❏ 500 g (1 lb 2 oz) zucchini (courgettes)
- ❏ 200 g (7 oz) eggplant (aubergine)
- ❏ 300 g (10½ oz) potatoes
- ❏ 300 g (10½ oz) broad beans in their shell or 100 g (3½ oz) shelled broad beans (e.g. frozen)
- ❏ 400 g (14 oz) green beans
- ❏ 50 g (1¾ oz) cucumber
- ❏ 2 garlic cloves
- ❏ 1 small bulb spring onion (scallion)
- ❏ 5–6 sprigs basil
- ❏ 1 sprig mint
- ❏ 500 g (1 lb 2 oz) peaches
- ❏ 500 g (1 lb 2 oz) apricots
- ❏ 500 g (1 lb 2 oz) strawberries

Refrigerated

- ❏ 100 g (3½ oz) sea bream fillet
- ❏ 100 g (3½ oz) veal steak
- ❏ 10–20 g (¼–¾ oz) emmental or cheddar cheese
- ❏ 50 ml (1½ fl oz) milk
- ❏ 3 small tubs yoghurt (to be supplemented according to your baby's needs)
- ❏ 10 g (¼ oz) butter

Groceries

- ❏ ½ vanilla bean
- ❏ a few drops of orange flower water
- ❏ 15 g (½ oz) very fine semolina

In the cupboard

- ❏ olive oil

Sunday

1. Prepare

🕐 20 mins

- Wash the fruit and vegetables.
- Peel the potatoes. Remove half the skin of the cucumber and zucchini, peeling in stripes. Trim the green beans, removing any strings. Slice the zucchini into rounds and cut the potatoes, cucumber and eggplant into cubes.
- Shell the broad beans. Remove their thin skins after dropping them into a bowl of boiling water for a few moments.
- Peel the tomatoes after dropping them into a bowl of boiling water as well. Roughly chop the tomatoes and remove most of the seeds (but save the juice).
- Rinse, dry and pick the basil and mint leaves.
- Peel the garlic cloves and finely chop or grate them. Peel the spring onion.
- Peel the peaches. Halve the peaches and apricots, remove their stones and slice. Hull the strawberries.
- Cut the veal into small pieces.

2. Cook

🕐 40 mins

PROTEIN Steam the fish fillet for 10–15 minutes and steam the veal for 30 minutes.

VEGETABLES Steam the vegetables (without mixing them), scattering over the grated or chopped garlic (set aside a good pinch for the gazpacho and baba ghanoush): 30–35 minutes for the potatoes, 10–15 minutes for the eggplant and zucchini, 10 minutes for the broad beans, 15–20 minutes for the green beans. Save the cooking water.

FRUITS Cook the peaches and apricots separately for about 15 minutes in a covered saucepan over fairly low heat, adding the seeds of the vanilla bean to the apricots.

3. Purée until smooth

 15 mins

VEGETABLES Purée the vegetables, adding enough cooking water each time to make it smooth. Set aside in bowls as you go:

RATATOUILLE 200 g (7 oz) zucchini + 100 g (3½ oz) eggplant + 100 g (3½ oz) tomato

ZUCCHINI + 5–6 basil leaves + 1 teaspoon olive oil

EGGPLANT + 1 teaspoon olive oil

BROAD BEANS + ½ teaspoon olive oil + 1–2 mint leaves

GREEN BEANS + 1 teaspoon butter + 5–6 basil leaves

TOMATOES (raw) + 2 teaspoons olive oil + 5–6 basil leaves

CUCUMBER + spring onion + 2–3 basil leaves + half the remaining garlic

MASHED POTATO + 1 teaspoon butter (don't purée it in a blender or food processor – it will become sticky and gluey)

FISH + 4–5 basil leaves + a little cooking water

VEAL + a little cooking water

FRUIT Purée the peaches, apricots and strawberries separately, adding a few drops of orange flower water to the peaches.

4. Weigh

 15 mins

Weigh out the purées for the week and put them into containers.

MONDAY → 10 g (¼ oz) sea bream + 200 g (7 oz) ratatouille
→ 100 g (3½ oz) peach
→ 50 g (1¾ oz) broad beans + 50 g (1¾ oz) green beans

TUESDAY → 10 g (¼ oz) veal + 50 g (1¾ oz) broad beans + 50 g (1¾ oz) zucchini + 50 g (1¾ oz) green beans + 50 g (1¾ oz) potato
→ 100 g (3½ oz) strawberries
→ 50 g (1¾ oz) cucumber + 50 g (1¾ oz) tomato (gazpacho)

WEDNESDAY → 100 g (3½ oz) tomato
→ 50 g (1¾ oz) peach + 50 g (1¾ oz) apricot
→ 100 g (3½ oz) zucchini

THURSDAY → 10 g (¼ oz) sea bream + 150 g (5½ oz) potato + 50 g (1¾ oz) tomato
→ 100 g (3½ oz) strawberries
→ 100 g (3½ oz) green beans

FRIDAY → 10 g (¼ oz) veal + 200 g (7 oz) ratatouille
→ 50 g (1¾ oz) strawberry + 50 g (1¾ oz) apricot
→ 100 g (3½ oz) tomato

BONUS RECIPE → 100 g (3½ oz) eggplant + 30 g (1 oz) tomato + remaining garlic

5. Store

STORING Clearly label → Monday's portions in the refrigerator and other portions in the freezer.

IMPORTANT: If you use frozen raspberries, consume them within 48 hours and don't refreeze them.

LEFTOVERS Freeze any extras in ice cube trays, which will make 10–20 g (¼–¾ oz) portions to use later, combined however you like. For the puréed bream and veal, weigh out 10 g (¼ oz) portions.

TIP You can use larger containers for the fruit purées, but they must be consumed within 48 hours after thawing. As your baby will be eating the same purée several times in a row, you can vary its flavour by adding the juice of an orange, for example.

If your baby isn't eating vegetables in the evening yet, you can still make the dinner portions and freeze them for later in 100 g (3½ oz) portions in containers or ice cube trays.

Ratatouille and sea bream / Peach purée / Broad and green bean soup with mint

🕐 Ready in 10 mins

LUNCH Reheat the sea bream and ratatouille.
SNACK Serve some peach purée.
DINNER Reheat the broad and green bean purées and add some water to make a soup-like consistency.

Veal and green vegetables /
Yoghurt and strawberry purée / Gazpacho

🕐 Ready in 10 mins

LUNCH Reheat the veal and vegetable purées.
SNACK Serve the strawberry purée poured over a tub of thick yoghurt.
DINNER Serve the cucumber and tomato gazpacho at room temperature.

Wednesday

Semolina and tomato / Peach and apricot purée / Zucchini and basil purée

🕐 Ready in 10 mins

LUNCH Make the semolina with cheese and tomato: finely grate the cheese. Heat 150 ml (5½ fl oz) water, pour in the semolina, stir and cook for 2–3 minutes to obtain a porridge-like consistency. Mix in 1–2 teaspoons cheese. Serve with the tomato purée (pour over or offer separately).
SNACK Offer some peach and apricot purée.
DINNER Reheat the zucchini and basil purée.

Sea bream, mashed potato and tomato purée / Strawberry smoothie / Green bean purée

🕐 Ready in 10 mins

LUNCH Reheat the sea bream, potato and tomato purées.
SNACK Whisk the strawberry purée with half a small tub of yoghurt and a little milk to thin out the mixture.
DINNER Reheat the green bean purée.

Friday

Veal and ratatouille / Strawberry and apricot purée / Tomato soup

🕐 Ready in 10 mins

LUNCH Reheat the veal and ratatouille.
SNACK Serve a strawberry and apricot purée.
DINNER Reheat the tomato purée and add some water to make a soup-like consistency.
It can also be served at room temperature.

Baba ghanoush

Ready in 10 mins

Mix the eggplant + tomato + garlic with 30 g (1 oz) yoghurt. Add it to a meal, or offer it on the weekend with a small serve of couscous for example. This is also a dish that can be adapted from an adult version.

Meal plans 6–9 months

sample week n°4

Timing

1 HR 30 MIN
IN THE KITCHEN

Season: autumn

In other seasons, replace the quince with pear or apple, and the clementines with raspberries.

Daily requirements*

Meat or fish: 10–15 g (¼–½ oz) at lunchtime

Vegetables: 120–300 g (4¼–10½ oz)

Fruit: build up gradually from 50 g (1¾ oz) to 130 g (4½ oz)

Milk and dairy products: 500–900 ml (17–31 fl oz)

*Check the recommendations of your paediatrician.

Monday
Beef, carrots and parsnip
Apple and quince purée
Zucchini and silverbeet soup

Tuesday
Tuna with curried sweet potato and zucchini
Yoghurt with apple and clementine purée
Parsnip and apple soup

Wednesday
Polenta and cheese with pumpkin purée
Apple and quince purée with yoghurt
Zucchini and herb purée

Thursday
Beef, pumpkin and silverbeet
Apple and clementine purée
Carrot and chervil purée

Friday
Sweet potato, zucchini and egg
Banana and yoghurt
Pumpkin, sweet potato and coconut soup

bonus recipe
Kiwifruit and banana smoothie

For storing

10 x 150 ml (5 fl oz) containers

4 x 250 ml (9 fl oz) containers

4 ice cube trays

Equipment

1 steamer

1 cast-iron pot or saucepan

1 blender or food processor for puréeing

shopping list

Fruit, vegetables and herbs

- ❏ 500 g (1 lb 2 oz) butternut pumpkin (or other variety)
- ❏ 500 g (1 lb 2 oz) zucchini (courgettes)
- ❏ 300 g (10½ oz) silverbeet
- ❏ 400 g (14 oz) sweet potato
- ❏ 400 g (14 oz) carrots
- ❏ 250 g (9 oz) parsnips
- ❏ 6–7 sprigs chervil or flat-leaf parsley
- ❏ ½ bunch chives
- ❏ 2–3 mint leaves
- ❏ 2 small red onions
- ❏ 2 garlic cloves
- ❏ a small piece fresh ginger
- ❏ 4 apples
- ❏ 3 quinces
- ❏ 6 clementines or small oranges
- ❏ 2 bananas
- ❏ 1 kiwifruit
- ❏ 1 lemon

Refrigerated

- ❏ 100 g (3½ oz) minced beef
- ❏ 20 g (¾ oz) butter
- ❏ 1 egg
- ❏ 10–15 g (¼–½ oz) emmental or cheddar cheese
- ❏ 100 g (3½ oz) line-caught tuna or bonito
- ❏ 100 ml (3½ fl oz) milk
- ❏ 3 small tubs yoghurt (to be supplemented according to your baby's needs)

Groceries

- ❏ 2 cloves
- ❏ ½ vanilla bean
- ❏ 1 tablespoon coconut milk
- ❏ 50 g (1¾ oz) fine semolina

In the cupboard

- ❏ olive oil
- ❏ sugar
- ❏ ground cinnamon
- ❏ a spice mix like curry powder or garam masala (not too spicy)

week n°4 Sunday

1. Prepare

🕐 20 mins

- Wash the fruit and vegetables.
- Peel the carrots, parsnips, pumpkin and sweet potatoes. Cut the sweet potatoes, parsnips and pumpkin into cubes. Slice the carrots and zucchini into rounds.
- For the silverbeet: cut the leaves and stems into strips.
- Peel and finely chop the onions and the garlic.
- Rinse and dry the chervil and chives, and pick the leaves from the chervil (the chives will be used twice and the chervil four times).
- Peel and core the apples, and cut them into slices. Peel the clementines and cut them into segments.

2. Cook

🕐 40 mins

FRUIT Cook the apples for 10–15 minutes, covered, over medium heat, with 1 tablespoon of water, 1 pinch cinnamon and two cloves. Simmer the quinces whole for 20 minutes. Once they have cooled, peel and core them.

VEGETABLES Set aside 1 tablespoon of raw carrots for the beef. Steam the vegetables (they can be cooked together, but don't mix them so you can take them out separately) or boil them, flavoured with a little finely chopped garlic and onion (set aside about ½ onion for the beef): 30–35 minutes for the sweet potato, parsnip, pumpkin and carrots, and about 10–15 minutes for the zucchini and silverbeet (the vegetables need to be tender). Save the cooking water.

PROTEIN Sauté the onion and carrot that you set aside in a small saucepan in 1 teaspoon butter and 1 teaspoon olive oil for 6–7 minutes. Add the beef and brown for 5 minutes. Add some of the vegetable cooking water (enough to cover the meat), cover and cook over low heat for 30 minutes.

Grate some ginger on the tuna (the equivalent of a large pinch) and steam for 30–35 minutes. It needs to be well cooked.

3. Purée until smooth

 15 mins

BEEF (with sautéed onion and carrot) + enough of the cooking juices to make a purée

TUNA (with ginger) + a few drops of olive oil + some cooking water

VEGETABLES Purée the cooked vegetables separately (with the garlic and onion that you cooked with them), adding a little of the cooking water (or plain water) and a small amount of oil or butter:

CARROTS + a little chervil + 1 teaspoon olive oil

ZUCCHINI + a little chervil and chives + 1 teaspoon olive oil

SWEET POTATO + 1 teaspoon butter + 1 pinch curry powder

PUMPKIN + 1 teaspoon butter + chervil and chives

SILVERBEET (leaves and stems together) + 2 teaspoons olive oil

PARSNIP + 1 tablespoon cooked apple + chervil + 1 teaspoon butter

FRUIT Purée the apples, clementines and quinces separately, adding the seeds of ½ vanilla bean to the quince. Strain the clementine purée to remove the thin membranes.

4. Weigh

 15 mins

Weigh out the purées for the week and put them into containers.

MONDAY → 10 g (¼ oz) beef + 50 g (1¾ oz) parsnip + 150 g (5½ oz) carrot
→ 50 g (1¾ oz) apple + 50 g (1¾ oz) quince
→ 50 g (1¾ oz) zucchini + 50 g (1¾ oz) silverbeet

TUESDAY → 10 g (¼ oz) tuna + 100 g (3½ oz) sweet potato + 100 g (3½ oz) zucchini
→ 50 g (1¾ oz) apple + 50 g (1¾ oz) clementine
→ 100 g (3½ oz) parsnip

WEDNESDAY → 100 g (3½ oz) pumpkin
→ 50 g (1¾ oz) apple + 50 g (1¾ oz) quince
→ 100 g (3½ oz) zucchini

THURSDAY → 10 g (¼ oz) beef + 150 g (5½ oz) pumpkin + 50 g (1¾ oz) silverbeet
→ 50 g (1¾ oz) apple + 50 g (1¾ oz) clementine
→ 100 g (3½ oz) carrot

FRIDAY → 100 g (3½ oz) sweet potato + 100 g (3½ oz) zucchini
→ 50 g (1¾ oz) sweet potato + 50 g (1¾ oz) pumpkin + 1 tablespoon coconut milk

5. Store

STORING Clearly label → Monday's portions in the refrigerator and other portions in the freezer.

TIP You can use larger containers for the fruit purées, but they must be consumed within 48 hours after thawing. As your baby will be eating the same purée several times in a row, you can vary its flavour by adding the juice of an orange, for example.

If your baby isn't eating vegetables in the evening yet, you can still make the dinner portions and freeze them for later in 100 g (3½ oz) portions in containers or ice cube trays.

LEFTOVERS Freeze any extras in ice cube trays, which will make 10–20 g (¼–¾ oz) portions to use later, combined however you like. For the puréed fish and beef, weigh out 10 g (¼ oz) portions.

Beef, carrots and parsnip / Apple and quince purée/ Zucchini and silverbeet soup

🕐 Ready in 10 mins

LUNCH Reheat the beef, carrot and parsnip purées.
SNACK Serve the apple and quince purée.
DINNER Reheat the zucchini and silverbeet purées and add some water to make a soup-like consistency.

Tuna with curried sweet potato and zucchini / Yoghurt with apple and clementine purée / Parsnip and apple soup

🕐 Ready in 10 mins

LUNCH Reheat the tuna, curried sweet potato and zucchini purées. When serving, you can offer them separately or make a little mixture.

SNACK Pour the clementine and apple purée over a yoghurt.

DINNER Reheat the parsnip and apple purée and and add some water to make a soup-like consistency.

Wednesday

Polenta and cheese with pumpkin purée /
Apple and quince purée with yoghurt / Zucchini and herb purée

🕐 Ready in 10 mins

LUNCH Reheat the pumpkin purée. For the polenta, heat 100 ml (3½ fl oz) milk. Take it off the heat and add 10 g (¼ oz) grated cheese and the polenta in a stream, stirring constantly. Keep stirring after you take it off the heat (the mixture will thicken). Serve with the pumpkin purée.

SNACK Serve an apple and quince purée and a small tub of yoghurt.

DINNER Gently reheat the zucchini and herb purée.

Beef, pumpkin and silverbeet / Apple and clementine purée / Carrot and chervil purée

🕐 Ready in 10 mins

LUNCH Reheat the beef, pumpkin and silverbeet purées.
SNACK Serve some apple and clementine purée.
DINNER Reheat the carrot and chervil purée.

Friday

Sweet potato, zucchini and egg / Banana and yoghurt / Pumpkin, sweet potato and coconut soup

Ready in 10 mins

LUNCH Reheat the sweet potato and zucchini purées. Cook a hard-boiled egg (8–9 minutes from when it reaches the boil). Mash a quarter of the egg and serve it with the puréed vegetables (give the rest of the egg to another member of the family).

SNACK Mash the banana into a yoghurt.

DINNER Reheat the pumpkin and sweet potato purées and add some water to make a soup-like consistency.

Kiwifruit and banana smoothie

🕙 Ready in 10 mins

Purée together 1 kiwifruit, ½ banana, 2–3 mint leaves (rinsed and dried) and a few drops of lemon juice: this a way to introduce kiwifruit to your baby, who is already familiar with banana. Other possibilities: replace the banana with cucumber or apple juice (without added sugar). Caution: if there is a predisposition to allergy, wait 12 months before offering kiwifruit.

Meal plans 9-12 months

sample week n°1

Timing

2 HRS
IN THE KITCHEN

Season: summer

In other seasons, replace the peaches, apricots and melon with apples, pears and bananas. Use tinned peeled tomatoes.

Daily requirements*

Meat or fish:
15–20 g (½–¾ oz) at lunchtime

Vegetables: 200–400 g (7–14 oz)

Fruit: 2 serves a day of purées (80–100 g/2¾–3½ oz) and/or thinly sliced fresh fruits

Milk and dairy products: 500–900 ml (17–31 fl oz)

Starchy foods:
50 g (1¼ oz) – cooked weight – in the evening

*Check the recommendations of your paediatrician.

Monday

Fish and ratatouille
Peach purée and yoghurt
Zucchini risotto

Tuesday

Chicken and green vegetables
Melon and orange flower yoghurt
Lentil, zucchini and spinach soup

Wednesday

Lentils and ratatouille with fromage frais
Cream cheese and raspberry coulis
Tomato soup

Thursday

Fish, mashed potato and zucchini
Mashed banana, yoghurt and cinnamon
Pasta with tomato and parmesan cheese

Friday

Chicken and green vegetables
with potatoes
Apricot smoothie
Zucchini, spinach and potato soup

bonus recipe

Porridge

For storing

10 x 150 ml (5 fl oz) containers
5 x 250 ml (9 fl oz) containers
4 ice cube trays

Equipment

1 steamer
2 saucepans
or cast-iron pots
1 blender or food processor for puréeing

shopping list

Fruit, vegetables and herbs

- ❏ 100 g (3½ oz) eggplant (aubergine)
- ❏ 900 g (2 lb) zucchini (courgettes)
- ❏ 600 g (1 lb 5 oz) tomatoes
- ❏ 400 g (14 oz) potatoes
- ❏ 600 g (1 lb 5 oz) baby spinach or 300 g (10½ oz) frozen spinach
- ❏ 300 g (10½ oz) green beans
- ❏ 125 g (4½ oz) fennel
- ❏ 1 French shallot
- ❏ 1–2 garlic cloves
- ❏ 2 sprigs thyme
- ❏ 4–5 sprigs basil
- ❏ 500 g (1 lb 2 oz) apricots
- ❏ 500 g (1 lb 2 oz) peaches
- ❏ 2 bananas
- ❏ some melon
- ❏ 125 g (4½ oz) raspberries

Refrigerated

- ❑ 80 g (2¾ oz) white fish fillets
- ❑ 60 g (2¼ oz) chicken breast fillet
- ❑ 20 g (¾ oz) butter
- ❑ 20–30 g (¾–1 oz) parmesan cheese
- ❑ 100 ml (3½ fl oz) milk
- ❑ 20 g (¾ oz) pasteurised fromage frais or cream cheese
- ❑ a little crème fraîche
- ❑ 60 g (2¼ oz) portion cream cheese or thick yoghurt + 4 small tubs yoghurt + (to be supplemented according to the age, tastes and appetite of your baby)

Groceries

- ❑ 15 g (½ oz) short-grain rice
- ❑ 50 g (1¾ oz) green lentils
- ❑ a few drops of orange flower water
- ❑ 1 vanilla bean
- ❑ 20 g (¾ oz) baby oat flakes (or special baby cereal)
- ❑ 1 organic salt-free vegetable stock cube
- ❑ 15 g (½ oz) small soup pasta

In the cupboard

- ❑ olive oil
- ❑ sugar
- ❑ ground cinnamon

Sunday

1. Prepare

🕐 20 mins

- Wash the vegetables. Peel the potatoes. (Don't peel the zucchini unless the skin is really thick.) Trim the green beans. Remove any damaged parts from the fennel. Dice the potatoes. Slice the zucchini into rounds and the eggplant into small cubes. Thinly slice the fennel.
- Peel the garlic. Peel and chop the French shallot.
- Peel the tomatoes: drop them into boiling water for 1 minute, then remove the skin and roughly chop.
- Rinse the spinach and discard any damaged leaves.
- Rinse and dry the herbs and pick off the leaves.
- Set aside some whole fruits to serve ripe. Peel the peaches, cut them in half, remove the stones and cut into slices (peel them using the same process as the tomatoes, with a quick bath in boiling water). Chop the apricots, removing the stones. Rinse the raspberries very briefly.
- Rinse the lentils.
- Dice the chicken.

2. Cook

🕐 50 mins

FRUITS Cook the peaches over medium heat, covered, with 2 tablespoons water and ½ split vanilla bean for 10–15 minutes. Cook the apricots in the same way.

FISH Steam the fish for 10–15 minutes.

CHICKEN Heat 2 teaspoons olive oil in a cast-iron pot. Add the shallot and cook for 5 minutes.

→ **HALF IN A BOWL** Add chicken and stir to lightly brown. Add the green beans, fennel and 200 g (7 oz) zucchini, stir for 1 minute, then add ½ glass water and 7–8 basil leaves, lower the heat and cook, covered, for 20 minutes. Add 100 g (3½ oz) spinach.

→ **BOWL**

RATATOUILLE Heat 2 teaspoons olive oil in the cast-iron pot over low heat. Add half of the garlic, let it flavour the oil for 2–3 minutes, then stir in the eggplant and cook for 7–8 minutes over medium heat. Add 300 g (10½ oz) zucchini, stir 3–4 minutes, then stir in 300 g (10½ oz) raw tomatoes, 10 basil leaves and the thyme. Cook for 10 minutes.

STEAMED VEGETABLES Steam the potatoes and the remaining zucchini for 30–35 minutes. Steam the rest of the fresh spinach for 15 minutes. Reserve the cooking water.

LENTILS Put the lentils in a saucepan and cover with four times their volume of water. Cook for 20 minutes and drain, reserving the cooking water.

3. Purée

 15 mins

RATATOUILLE

CHICKEN AND GREEN VEGETABLES

STEAMED ZUCCHINI + SPINACH + 2 teaspoons olive oil + a few basil leaves + reserved cooked shallot

RAW TOMATOES + 2 teaspoons olive oil + a few basil leaves + remaining garlic

LENTILS + a little cooking water + 1 teaspoon olive oil

POTATO Mash using a potato masher or fork with 10 g (¼ oz) butter and a little milk (avoid using a blender as the potatoes will become gluey).

FISH Check that it doesn't contain any bones, and remove them carefully if it does. Purée (add a little water or vegetable cooking water if necessary).

FRUIT Purée the peaches, apricots and raspberries separately. Add 1 pinch sugar + a little water to the raspberries to obtain the consistency of coulis, setting aside a few whole raspberries.

OAT FLAKES almost to the consistency of a powder.

4. Weigh

 15 mins

Weigh out the purées for the week and put them into containers.

MONDAY → 15 g (½ oz) fish + 200 g (7 oz) ratatouille
→ 100 g (3½ oz) peach
→ 100 g (3½ oz) zucchini and spinach

TUESDAY → 200 g (7 oz) chicken and green vegetables
→ 50 g (1¾ oz) lentils + 50 g (1¾ oz) zucchini and spinach

WEDNESDAY → 150 g (5½ oz) ratatouille + 50 g (1¾ oz) lentils + 20 g (¾ oz) fromage frais
→ 100 g (3½ oz) raspberry coulis
→ 50 g (1¾ oz) tomato + 50 g (1¾ oz) potato

THURSDAY → 15 g (½ oz) fish + 100 g (3½ oz) potato + 100 g (3½ oz) zucchini and spinach
→ 100 g (3½ oz) tomato

FRIDAY → 150 g (5½ oz) chicken and green vegetables + 50 g (1¾ oz) potato
→ 100 g (3½ oz) apricot
→ 50 g (1¾ oz) zucchini and spinach + 50 g (1¾ oz) potato

BONUS RECIPE → 100 g (3½ oz) peach

5. Store

STORING Clearly label → Monday's portions in the refrigerator and other portions in the freezer.

LEFTOVERS Freeze any extras in ice cube trays to make 10–20 g (¼– ¾ oz) portions. For the fish, weigh out 15 g (½ oz) portions. For the chicken, weigh out a 200 g (7 oz) portion (because there are also vegetables in it). → **FREEZER**

Fish and ratatouille / Peach purée and yoghurt/ Zucchini risotto

🕐 Ready in 10 mins (15 minutes for dinner)

LUNCH Reheat the ratatouille and fish purées. Offer a few fresh raspberries for dessert.
SNACK Serve some peach purée with a yoghurt.
DINNER Crumble and dissolve ¼ vegetable stock cube in 300 ml (10½ fl oz) hot water. In a saucepan, stir the rice in 10 g (¼ oz) melted butter until it looks translucent. Gradually add the stock, stirring in each addition and waiting until it has been absorbed. Once the rice is tender, add 10 g (¼ oz) grated parmesan cheese, a small teaspoon crème fraîche and the zucchini and spinach purée.

Chicken and green vegetables / Melon and orange flower yoghurt / Lentil, zucchini and spinach soup

🕐 Ready in 10 mins

LUNCH Reheat the chicken and vegetables. Offer some apricot purée for dessert.
SNACK Purée a piece of melon, or offer it in pieces. Mix a yoghurt with a tiny pinch of sugar and a few drops of orange flower water.
DINNER Reheat the container of lentils with zucchini and spinach and add some water to make a soup-like consistency.

Lentils and ratatouille with fromage frais /
Cream cheese and raspberry coulis / Tomato soup

🕐 Ready in 10 mins

LUNCH Reheat the container of lentils and ratatouille. Offer pieces of melon for dessert.
SNACK Pour some raspberry coulis over a cream cheese portion or thick yoghurt.
DINNER Reheat the tomato purée and mashed potato and add some water to make a soup-like consistency.
Top with a little parmesan cheese. You can give your baby a small piece of bread to chew.

Fish, mashed potato and zucchini / Mashed banana, yoghurt and cinnamon / Pasta with tomato and parmesan cheese

🕐 Ready in 10 mins

LUNCH Reheat the fish and potato with zucchini. Offer pieces of peach for dessert.

SNACK Offer a banana mashed into some yoghurt with a little ground cinnamon.

DINNER Cook the pasta and serve with the tomato purée and some grated parmesan cheese.

Chicken and green vegetables with potatoes /
Apricot smoothie / Zucchini, spinach and potato soup

🕐 Ready in 10 mins

LUNCH Reheat the chicken and vegetables and mashed potato and offer some pieces of banana for dessert.
SNACK Blend some apricot purée with a yoghurt.
DINNER Reheat the zucchini and spinach purée with the mashed potato and add some water to make
a soup-like consistency. Serve with a piece of bread to nibble.

Porridge

🕐 Ready in 10 mins

From the age of 10 months, use regular rolled oats. Before then, use special baby cereals.
Heat 90 ml (3 fl oz) milk. Once it comes to a simmer, pour in the ground oat flakes in a stream.
Stir for 1 minute over medium heat, then lower the heat and cook for 3–4 minutes over low
heat. Serve with 1 pinch ground cinnamon and a little peach purée.

Meal plans 9–12 months

sample week n°2

Timing
2 HRS
IN THE KITCHEN

Season: autumn

In other seasons, use peeled tinned tomatoes. Replace the plums with pears.

Daily requirements*

Meat or fish: 15–20 g (½–¾ oz) at lunchtime

Vegetables: 200–400 g (7–14 oz)

Fruit: 2 serves a day of purées (80–100 g/ 2¾–3½ oz) and/or thinly sliced fresh fruits

Milk and dairy products: 500–900 ml (17–31 fl oz)

Starchy foods: 50 g (1¾ oz) – cooked weight – in the evening

*Check the recommendations of your paediatrician.

Monday
Beef and tomato stew with potatoes
Apple and plum purée with cream cheese
Rice and broccoli purée

Tuesday
Cod with herb and lemon crust
and broccoli purée
Plum smoothie
Pasta and tomato sauce

Wednesday
Spinach, mashed potato and egg
Apple and plum purée with dairy
Pumpkin, carrot and coconut stew

Thursday
Salmon, pumpkin and spinach
Banana and yoghurt
Corn and tomato soup

Friday
Beef and mashed potato with vegetables
Semolina pudding
Pasta and broccoli

bonus recipe
Pancakes

For storing

8 x 150 ml (5 fl oz) containers

7 x 250 ml (9 fl oz) containers

4 ice cube trays

Equipment

1 steamer
1 saucepan
1 ovenproof dish
1 blender or food processor for puréeing

shopping list

Fruit, vegetables and herbs

- ❏ 700 g (1 lb 9 oz) broccoli
- ❏ 700 g (1 lb 9 oz) tomatoes
- ❏ 500 g (1 lb 2 oz) potatoes
- ❏ 400 g (14 oz) corn cobs
- ❏ 400 g (14 oz) carrots
- ❏ 400 g (14 oz) frozen spinach or 1 kg (2 lb 4 oz) fresh
- ❏ 400 g (14 oz) pumpkin
- ❏ 1 leek
- ❏ 3 onions
- ❏ 1 garlic clove
- ❏ 1 small French shallot
- ❏ 5–6 sprigs basil
- ❏ 5–6 sprigs thyme
- ❏ a small piece fresh ginger
- ❏ 600 g (1 lb 5 oz) apples
- ❏ 500 g (1 lb 2 oz) plums
- ❏ 1 small pineapple
- ❏ 1 organic or untreated lemon
- ❏ 1 banana
- ❏ 1 pear

Refrigerated

- ❏ 50 g (1¾ oz) minced beef
- ❏ 50 g (1¾ oz) cod fillet or other white fish
- ❏ 2 eggs
- ❏ 30 g (1 oz) parmesan cheese
- ❏ 50 g (1¾ oz) wild salmon fillet
- ❏ 130 ml (4 fl oz) milk
- ❏ 2 small tubs yoghurt + 60 g (2¼ oz) portion cream cheese or thick yoghurt (to be supplemented according to your baby's needs)
- ❏ 1 teaspoon crème fraîche
- ❏ 50 g (1¾ oz) butter

Groceries

- ❏ 4 melba toasts or rusks
- ❏ 15 g (½ oz) short-grain rice
- ❏ 30 g (1 oz) small pasta shapes
- ❏ 60 g (2¼ oz) plain flour
- ❏ ½ vanilla bean
- ❏ 110 ml (3½ fl oz) coconut milk
- ❏ 1 organic salt-free vegetable stock cube
- ❏ 1 star anise
- ❏ 15 g (½ oz) semolina

In the cupboard

- ❏ olive or canola oil
- ❏ sweet paprika
- ❏ ground cumin
- ❏ ground cinnamon
- ❏ mild curry powder
- ❏ sugar

Sunday

1. Prepare

🕐 20 mins

- Wash the vegetables. Peel the carrots and potatoes. Cut the broccoli into small florets, slice the carrots into rounds and cut the potatoes into cubes. Cut the pumpkin in half, remove the seeds and cut into cubes (it is not essential to peel it). Trim the green ends of the leek, split it in half lengthways almost all the way down and rinse it well, then thinly slice.
- Peel the tomatoes: drop them in a bowl of boiling water for a few moments, then remove the skin. Chop them roughly.
- Slice the corn kernels off the cob with a knife.
- Rinse the spinach (if not frozen) and remove any tough stems and damaged leaves.
- Peel and finely chop the onions. Peel the garlic.
- Rinse and dry the thyme (if fresh) and basil, and pick the leaves.
- Wash and peel the apples, remove the cores and cut into slices.
- Wash the plums and remove the stones.
- Peel the pineapple, cut it in 4 lengthways and remove the tough middle section. Cut into pieces.

2. Cook

🕐 50 mins

FRUIT Cook each fruit separately for 10–15 minutes, covered, over medium heat, with 1 tablespoon water: apples + 1 pinch cinnamon; plums + 1 star anise; pineapple + 1 pinch sugar + ½ vanilla bean (➜ remove the bean and add the scraped-out seeds).

FLAVOUR BASE Sweat the onions, the leek and the equivalent of 1 carrot with 1 large pinch thyme leaves in a small saucepan with 2 teaspoons oil and 10 g (¼ oz) butter, for 7–8 minutes. ➜ **THREE-QUARTERS IN A BOWL**

BEEF In the same saucepan, add the beef and cook, stirring, until brown. Add 200 g (7 oz) tomatoes and 5–6 basil leaves, and simmer over low heat for 10 minutes. ➜ **BOWL**

FISH Preheat the oven to 190°C (375°F). Crush the melba toasts in a food processor with 1 teaspoon thyme, 10 basil leaves and 1 pinch grated lemon zest. Put the fish in an ovenproof dish and sprinkle with the herb mixture. Melt 15 g (½ oz) butter, add 1 tablespoon lemon juice and sprinkle over the fish. Cook for 10–15 minutes.

VEGETABLES Heat two-thirds of the rest of the flavour base in the saucepan. Grate in a little garlic, add the rest of the tomatoes and 5–6 basil leaves, stir and simmer for 10–15 minutes over low heat. ➜**BOWL** Put the rest of the flavour base in the saucepan over medium heat, add the pumpkin, carrot, ¼ teaspoon grated ginger, the same amount of garlic and 1 pinch curry powder. Stir for 2–3 minutes, then add 60 ml (2 fl oz) coconut milk, ½ vegetable stock cube and enough water to half cover. Cover and cook for 20–25 minutes.

Steam the remaining vegetables until tender: the broccoli will take 15–20 minutes, the spinach will take 10 minutes and the potatoes will take 30–35 minutes. Save the cooking water.

3. Purée

🕐 15 mins

BEEF + all its cooking sauce

FISH Check it doesn't contain any bones, and remove them carefully if it does. Purée the salmon and cod separately (add a little water or vegetable cooking water if necessary).

PUMPKIN, CARROT AND COCONUT STEW

COOKED TOMATO (half)

COOKED TOMATO (the other half) + corn + 1 pinch paprika + 1 pinch cumin

Purée the other vegetables separately, adding a little cooking water (or plain water) and a small amount of oil or butter to make purées:

BROCCOLI + 5–6 basil leaves + 1 teaspoon olive oil

SPINACH + 10 g (¼ oz) butter

POTATO Mash using a potato masher or fork with 10 g (¼ oz) butter and a little milk until smooth.

FRUIT Purée the plums (remove star anise), apples and pineapple separately.

4. Weigh

🕐 15 mins

Weigh out the purées for the week and put them into containers.

MONDAY ➜ 50 g (1¾ oz) beef and tomato stew + 150 g (5½ oz) potato
➜ 100 g (3½ oz) apple + 100 g (3½ oz) plum*
➜ 100 g (3½ oz) broccoli

TUESDAY ➜ 15 g (½ oz) cod + 200 g (7 oz) broccoli
➜ 100 g (3½ oz) plum
➜ 100 g (3½ oz) tomato

WEDNESDAY ➜ 100 g (3½ oz) potato + 100 g (3½ oz) spinach
➜ 100 g (3½ oz) pumpkin, carrot and coconut stew

THURSDAY ➜ 15 g (½ oz) salmon + 150 g (5½ oz) pumpkin, carrot and coconut stew + 50 g (1¾ oz) spinach
➜ 100 g (3½ oz) tomato and corn

FRIDAY ➜ 50 g (1¾ oz) beef and tomato stew + 50 g (1¾ oz) potato + 50 g (1¾ oz) spinach + 50 g (1¾ oz) pumpkin, carrot and coconut stew
➜ 100 g (3½ oz) broccoli

LUNCHTIME DESSERTS ➜ 100 g (3½ oz) pineapple
➜ 100 g (3½ oz) apple + 100 g (3½ oz) pineapple*
➜ 100 g (3½ oz) apple

*These large containers of fruit contain several servings; they are intended for at least two meals. If you prefer, you can divide into 100 g (3½ oz) portions (= 1 meal) in 150 ml (5 fl oz) containers.

5. Store

STORING Clearly label ➜ Monday's portions in the refrigerator and other portions in the freezer.

LEFTOVERS Freeze any extras in ice cube trays to make 10–20 g (¼–¾ oz) portions. For the fish, weigh out 15 g (½ oz) portions. For the beef, weigh out 70–80 g (2½–2¾ oz) portions (because it also contains tomato). ➜ **FREEZER**

Beef and tomato stew with potatoes / Apple and plum purée with cream cheese / Rice and broccoli purée

🕐 Ready in 10 minutes (20 minutes for dinner)

LUNCH Reheat the beef and tomato stew and potato. Offer small cut pieces of ripe pear for dessert.

SNACK Serve an apple and plum purée with a cream cheese portion or thick yoghurt.

DINNER Heat 300 ml (10½ fl oz) water with ½ crumbled stock cube. Peel and finely chop the shallot, soften it for 5 minutes over low heat in 1 teaspoon butter, add 15 g (½ oz) rice and stir. Gradually add the stock, stirring, until the rice is cooked (about 20 minutes). Add ½ teaspoon crème fraîche and 10 g (¼ oz) grated parmesan cheese. Reheat the broccoli purée and mix it into the rice. If your baby isn't ready for the texture of rice yet, you can purée it.

Tuesday

week n°2

Cod with herb and lemon crust and broccoli purée / Plum smoothie / Pasta and tomato sauce

🕐 Ready in 10 mins

LUNCH Reheat the cod and broccoli purées. Offer some apple purée for dessert.
SNACK Process 70–100 g (2½–3½ oz) yoghurt with the plum purée.
DINNER Cook 15 g (½ oz) pasta. Meanwhile, reheat the tomato purée. Serve with 10 g (¼ oz) grated parmesan cheese. If your baby isn't ready for the texture of pasta yet, you can purée it.

Spinach, mashed potato and egg / Apple and plum purée with dairy / Pumpkin, carrot and coconut stew

🕐 Ready in 10 mins

LUNCH Boil an egg for 9 minutes. Reheat the potato and spinach purées. Mash and serve half the boiled egg with this purée. Offer some pineapple purée for dessert.
SNACK Serve an apple and pineapple purée with a serve of dairy.
DINNER Reheat the pumpkin, carrot and coconut stew.

Salmon, pumpkin and spinach / Banana and yoghurt / Corn and tomato soup

🕐 Ready in 10 mins

LUNCH Reheat the salmon and spinach purées and the pumpkin, carrot and coconut stew. Offer some apple purée for dessert.

SNACK Serve a yoghurt and a banana cut into small pieces (once your baby likes to hold the pieces and can chew on them).

DINNER Reheat the tomato and corn purée and add some water to make a soup-like consistency.

Beef and mashed potato with vegetables / Semolina pudding / Pasta and broccoli

Ready in 15 mins

LUNCH Reheat the beef with the mashed potato and vegetables and offer a fruit purée for dessert.

SNACK Heat 100 ml (3½ fl oz) milk. Pour in about 15 g (½ oz) fine semolina in a stream and stir well over very low heat until it is quite thick (it will happen quickly). You can serve with a little of your choice of fruit purée.

DINNER Cook 15 g (½ oz) pasta. Reheat the broccoli purée. Serve with 10 g (¼ oz) grated parmesan cheese. If your baby isn't ready for the texture of pasta yet, you can purée it.

Pancakes
(for babies who can already chew)

🕐 Ready in 15 mins

Mix the flour with 50 ml (1½ fl oz) coconut milk (can be replaced with milk, almond milk or even water) and 1 egg; whisk together well. Cook small ladlefuls of this batter in a hot frying pan greased with butter. Brown the pancakes well on each side.

Meal plans 9-12 months

sample
week
n°3

Timing

2 HRS
IN THE KITCHEN

Season:
winter

In other seasons, replace
the watercress with
baby spinach
and the clementines
with strawberries.

Daily
requirements*

Meat or fish:
15–20 g (½–¾ oz)
at lunchtime

Vegetables: 200–400 g
(7–14 oz)

Fruit: 2 serves a day
of purées (80–100 g/
2¾–3½ oz) and/or thinly
sliced fresh fruits

Milk and dairy products:
500–900 ml (17–31 fl oz)

Starchy foods:
50 g (1¾ oz) – cooked
weight – in the evening

*Check the recommendations
of your paediatrician.

Monday

Duck à l'orange with carrot, celeriac
and turnip purée
Apple purée and yoghurt
Potato and leek soup

Tuesday

Orange fish and mashed potato
with watercress
Apple mousse
Carrot, celeriac and turnip soup

Wednesday

Vegetable stew with almonds and egg
Fruit salad
Pasta with watercress and cheese

Thursday

Duck and mashed potato with watercress
Semolina pudding with orange flower water
Potato and leek soup

Friday

Fish and vegetable stew
Yoghurt and banana
Polenta and cheese

bonus recipe

Sponge fingers

For storing

4 x 150 ml (5 fl oz)
containers

6 x 250 ml (9 fl oz)
containers

4 ice cube trays

Equipment

1 steamer

1 large saucepan

2 saucepans
or cast-iron pots

2 small ovenproof dishes
with a lid (or foil)

1 blender or food
processor for puréeing

shopping list

Fruit, vegetables and herbs

- ❏ 300 g (10½ oz) celeriac
- ❏ 300 g (10½ oz) turnips
- ❏ 500 g (1 lb 2 oz) potatoes
- ❏ 700 g (1 lb 9 oz) carrots
- ❏ ½ bunch watercress
- ❏ 1 garlic clove
- ❏ 400 g (14 oz) leek
- ❏ 10 sprigs coriander (cilantro)
- ❏ 3 sprigs flat-leaf parsley
- ❏ 2 onions
- ❏ 3 pears
- ❏ 3 clementines or mandarins
- ❏ 4 apples
- ❏ 2 bananas
- ❏ 3 oranges
- ❏ 2 organic or untreated lemons

Chilled sectionn

- ❏ 100 g (3½ oz) duck breast
- ❏ 100 g (3½ oz) white fish fillet
- ❏ 60 g (2¼ oz) butter
- ❏ 35 g (1¼ oz) emmental or cheddar cheese
- ❏ 250 ml (9 fl oz) milk
- ❏ 2 eggs
- ❏ 4 small tubs yoghurt (to be supplemented according to the age, tastes and appetite of your baby)

Groceries

- ❏ 50 g (1¾ oz) ground almonds
- ❏ ½ organic salt-free vegetable stock cube
- ❏ ½ vanilla bean
- ❏ a few drops of orange flower water
- ❏ 15 g (½ oz) polenta
- ❏ 15 g (½ oz) fine semolina
- ❏ 25 g (1 oz) small pasta shapes
- ❏ 60 g (2¼ oz) plain flour
- ❏ 1 pinch baking powder
- ❏ 30 g (1 oz) red lentils

In the cupboard

- ❏ olive oil
- ❏ curry powder
- ❏ sugar
- ❏ honey

Sunday

1. Prepare

🕐 20 mins

- Wash the vegetables. Peel the carrots, potatoes, turnips and celeriac. Slice the carrots into rounds and cut the potatoes, turnips and celeriac into cubes. Trim the ends of the leeks, split lengthways almost all the way down to thoroughly rinse out any dirt and slice them thinly.
- Rinse and pick over the watercress, removing any thick stems. Rinse and dry the parsley and coriander, then pick the leaves.
- Peel and finely chop the onions. Peel and grate the garlic.
- Rinse the lentils.
- Squeeze two oranges and a lemon, keeping the juices separate.
- Wash and peel the apples, remove the cores and cut into slices.

2. Cook

🕐 50 mins

FRUIT Cook the apples for 10–15 minutes, covered, over medium heat, with 1 tablespoon of water + the seeds of ½ vanilla bean.

FLAVOUR BASE Sweat the onions, 150 g (5½ oz) carrot and 100 g (3½ oz) leek in 2 teaspoons oil and 10 g (¼ oz) butter in a cast-iron pot for 7–8 minutes or until very tender. Add the garlic and mix well. ➜ **TWO-THIRDS IN A BOWL, LEAVE THE REST IN THE POT**

VEGETABLES Add ½ teaspoon curry powder to the vegetables in the pot and stir well. Add 200 g (7 oz) each of carrot, celeriac, turnip and potato and the ground almonds*, and stir well. Add the crumbled stock cube, the red lentils and some water to half cover the vegetables. Cover with a lid and cook over low heat for about 30–35 minutes. Put half of the remaining flavour base in a cast-iron pot, add the remaining carrot, celeriac and turnip, and stir well. Add some water to half cover the vegetables and cook for 15–20 minutes. ➜ **BOWL**

Add the rest of the flavour base to the pot with the rest of the potatoes and some water to cover; cook for 20–25 minutes. Set aside half the cooked potatoes in a bowl, add the watercress and mix together. Add the remaining leek to the pot and cook for 10 minutes.

PROTEIN Preheat the oven to 190°C (375°F). Place the fish and duck in separate ovenproof dishes with a lid (or use foil). Sprinkle the fish with 1 tablespoon olive oil, 1 tablespoon orange juice, 1 teaspoon lemon juice and half the coriander. Sprinkle the duck with 2 tablespoons orange juice, ½ teaspoon honey and 2 teaspoons olive oil. Cover the dishes and cook for 10–15 minutes. Take the fish out of the oven and continue cooking the duck at 130°C (250°F) for about 30–40 minutes. Remove the skin.

* If there is a predisposition to allergies, replace the ground almonds with 50 ml (1½ fl oz) coconut milk.

3. Purée

 15 mins

Depending on the tastes and teething stage of your baby, you don't have to purée foods as finely at this stage (even just mash some vegetables with a spoon).

DUCK + cooking sauce

FISH Check that it doesn't contain any bones, and remove them carefully if it does. Purée in a blender or food processor with its cooking juices (add a little water or vegetable cooking water if necessary).

VEGETABLE STEW WITH ALMONDS + the other half of the coriander

CARROT, CELERIAC AND TURNIP STEW + flat-leaf parsley

POTATO AND WATERCRESS Put through a food mill + 10 g (¼ oz) butter (or purée briefly with a hand blender – don't overdo it or the potato will become gluey).

POTATO AND LEEK Put through a food mill + 10 g (¼ oz) butter.

FRUITS Purée the apples.

4. Weigh

 15 mins

Weigh out the purées for the week and put them into containers.

MONDAY ➔ 15 g (½ oz) duck + 200 g (7 oz) carrot, celeriac and turnip stew
➔ 200 g (7 oz) apple*
➔ 100 g (3½ oz) potato and leek

TUESDAY ➔ 15 g (½ oz) fish + 200 g (7 oz) potato and watercress
➔ 100 g (3½ oz) carrot, celeriac and turnip stew

WEDNESDAY ➔ 200 g (7 oz) vegetable stew with almonds
➔ 50 g (1¾ oz) potato and watercress

THURSDAY ➔ 15 g (½ oz) duck + 200 g (7 oz) potato and watercress
➔ 100 g (3½ oz) potato and leek

FRIDAY ➔ 15 g (½ oz) fish + 200 g (7 oz) vegetable stew with almonds

* This large container contains several serves of apple purée – it should be enough for at least two meals. If you prefer, you can divide into 100 g (3½ oz) portions (= 1 meal) in 150 ml (5½ fl oz) containers.

5. Store

STORING Clearly label ➔ Monday's portions in the refrigerator and other portions in the freezer.
LEFTOVERS Freeze any extras in ice cube trays to make 10–20 g (¼–¾ oz) portions. For the fish and duck, weigh out 15 g (½ oz) portions. ➔ **FREEZER**

Duck à l'orange with carrot, celeriac and turnip purée / Apple purée and yoghurt / Potato and leek soup

⏱ Ready in 10 mins

LUNCH Reheat the duck and vegetables. Offer small pieces of ripe pear for dessert, once your baby is able to chew a little (otherwise, purée the pear).

SNACK Serve some apple purée with a yoghurt.

DINNER Heat the potato and leek purée and mix with a little milk to obtain the desired consistency.

Orange fish and mashed potato with watercress / Apple mousse / Carrot, celeriac and turnip soup

Ready in 10 mins

LUNCH Reheat the fish and potato with watercress. Offer segments of clementine for dessert.
SNACK Process 70–100 g (2½–3½ oz) yoghurt with 100 g (3½ oz) apple purée to make an instant apple mousse.
DINNER Heat the vegetable stew and add some water to make a soup-like consistency. You can offer a chunk of bread to nibble with it.

Wednesday

Vegetable stew with almonds and egg /
Fruit salad / Pasta with watercress and cheese

🕐 Ready in 15 mins

LUNCH Boil an egg for 9 minutes. Reheat the portion of vegetable stew. Serve half a hard-boiled egg, mashed, with the stew. For dessert you could offer a yoghurt.

SNACK Make a mini fruit salad with small cut pieces of banana, completely peeled and chopped segments of clementine and small pieces of pear, and sprinkle with the juice of an orange.

DINNER Cook the pasta. Reheat the mashed potato with watercress and serve with the pasta as if it were a sauce, adding about 15 g (½ oz) grated cheese.

Duck and mashed potato with watercress / Semolina pudding with orange flower water / Potato and leek soup

🕐 Ready in 10 mins

LUNCH Reheat the duck with the potato and watercress. Offer small pieces of pear for dessert.
SNACK Heat 100 ml (3½ fl oz) milk, add a few drops of orange flower water, pour in about 15 g (½ oz) fine semolina in a stream and stir well over very low heat until it is quite thick (it will happen quickly). You can very lightly sweeten the semolina with sugar or a little fruit purée.
DINNER Heat the potato and leek and add some water to make a soup-like consistency. Add 10 g (¼ oz) cubed or grated cheese.

Fish and vegetable stew /
Yoghurt and banana / Polenta and cheese

🕐 Ready in 10 mins

LUNCH Reheat the fish and vegetable stew. Offer a clementine that's completely peeled of rind and membranes for dessert.

SNACK Offer a mashed banana with yoghurt.

DINNER Heat 120 ml (3¾ fl oz) milk and pour in about 20 g (¾ oz) polenta in a stream. Stir well over very low heat until it is quite thick (it will happen quickly) and add 10 g (¼ oz) grated cheese.

Sponge fingers

(for babies who can already chew)

🕐 Ready in 20 mins

Preheat the oven to 160°C (320°F). Melt 30 g (1 oz) butter and allow to cool. Grate a little lemon zest very finely, about a pinch, mix it with 2 tablespoons sugar and add 2 teaspoons lemon juice. Mix in an egg. Add 60 g (2¼ oz) plain flour and 1 pinch baking powder, mix, then add the melted butter and 2 teaspoons olive oil. Place long spoonfuls on a baking tray covered with baking paper and bake for about 10 minutes.

Meal plans 9–12 months

Timing

2 HRS
IN THE KITCHEN

Season: spring

In other seasons, replace the strawberries with bananas and the asparagus with broad beans or green beans.

Daily requirements*

Meat or fish:
15–20 g (½–¾ oz) at lunchtime

Vegetables: 200–400 g
(7–14 oz)

Fruit: 2 serves a day of purées (80–100 g/
2¾–3½ oz) and/or thinly sliced fresh fruits

Milk and dairy products:
500–900 ml (17–31 fl oz)

Starchy foods:
50 g (1¾ oz) – cooked weight – in the evening

*Check the recommendations of your paediatrician.

Monday

Veal navarin
Apple purée with yoghurt
Asparagus and pea risotto

Tuesday

Sole fish cakes
Apple and rhubarb mousse
Pasta and tomato sauce

Wednesday

Zucchini and parmesan flan
Rice pudding
Carrot and coriander soup
with fromage frais

Thursday

Veal and mashed potato
Strawberry smoothie
Pasta with peas

Friday

Sole with chervil and zucchini
Rice pudding with apple
and strawberry purée
Green lentil and zucchini soup

bonus recipe

Muffins

For storing

11 x 150 ml (5 fl oz)
containers

6 x 250 ml (9 fl oz)
containers

4 ice cube trays

Equipment

1 steamer

2 saucepans or
cast-iron pots

1 small ovenproof dish
with a lid (or foil)

1 blender or food
processor for puréeing

1 frying pan

Fruit, vegetables and herbs

- ❏ 1 kg (2 lb 4 oz) zucchini (courgettes)
- ❏ 200 g (7 oz) asparagus
- ❏ 200 g (7 oz) shelled peas (fresh or frozen) or about 600 g (1 lb 5 oz) unshelled
- ❏ 100 g (3½ oz) turnips
- ❏ 300 g (10½ oz) carrots
- ❏ 200 g (7 oz) potatoes
- ❏ 2 bulb spring onions (scallions)
- ❏ 1–2 sprigs chervil or flat-leaf parsley
- ❏ 1 sprig mint
- ❏ 6 sprigs coriander (cilantro)
- ❏ 1 French shallot
- ❏ 400 g (14 oz) rhubarb
- ❏ 1 orange
- ❏ 5 apples
- ❏ 500 g (1 lb 2 oz) strawberries

Refrigerated

- ❏ 60 g (2¼ oz) veal steak
- ❏ 1 egg
- ❏ 60 g (2¼ oz) parmesan cheese
- ❏ 10 g (¼ oz) crème fraîche
- ❏ 50 g (1¾ oz) butter
- ❏ 70 ml (2¼ fl oz) milk
- ❏ 100 g (3½ oz) fillet of sole or other white fish
- ❏ 50 g (1¾ oz) pasteurised fromage frais or cream cheese
- ❏ 4 small tubs yoghurt (to be supplemented according to the age, tastes and appetite of your baby)

Groceries

- ❏ 40 g (1½ oz) risotto rice
- ❏ 20 g (¾ oz) green lentils
- ❏ 400 g (14 oz) tin tomatoes
- ❏ 1 organic salt-free vegetable stock cube
- ❏ 60 g (2¼ oz) small pasta shapes
- ❏ ½ vanilla bean
- ❏ 1 pinch baking powder
- ❏ 50 g (1¾ oz) plain flour

In the cupboard

- ❏ olive oil
- ❏ 65 g (2¼ oz) sugar

week n°4 Sunday

1. Prepare

🕐 20 mins

- Wash the vegetables. Peel the carrot, potato and turnip. Slice the carrots and zucchini into rounds and cut the potatoes and turnips into cubes. Remove the tough ends of the asparagus spears, then cut into short lengths.
- Peel and finely chop the spring onions. Rinse and dry the mint, chervil and coriander, and pick the leaves.
- Rinse the lentils.
- Rinse and hull the strawberries.
- Wash, trim and thinly slice the rhubarb.
- Wash and peel the apples, remove the cores and cut into slices.
- Dice the veal.

2. Cook

🕐 50 mins

FRUIT Cook the apples in a covered saucepan with 1 tablespoon water over medium heat for 10–15 minutes.

Preheat the oven to 180°C (350°F). Place the rhubarb in an ovenproof dish, sprinkle with the juice of ½ orange and 60 g (2¼ oz) sugar, cover with foil and cook for 20 minutes.

MEAT In a cast-iron pot or saucepan, brown the veal over medium heat in 2 teaspoons oil and 10 g (¼ oz) butter. Remove from the pan, add the spring onion and sweat for 5–6 minutes over low heat. Add 100 g (3½ oz) carrot, 200 g (7 oz) zucchini, 50 g (1¾ oz) turnip, 100 g (3½ oz) peas and 50 g (1¾ oz) asparagus and stir well. Cook over medium heat for 5 minutes, stirring regularly, then return the veal to the pan. Sprinkle with 10 g (¼ oz) flour. Add some water to half cover the ingredients and crumble in ½ vegetable stock cube. Cover and gently simmer for about 30–35 minutes until everything is cooked through but not falling apart.

FISH Steam the sole for 10 minutes.

VEGETABLES Steam all the remaining vegetables, without mixing together: carrot and turnip for 25 minutes, potatoes for 30–35 minutes, asparagus, zucchini and peas for 10–15 minutes.

LENTILS Put the lentils in a saucepan and cover with four times their volume of water. Cook for 20 minutes and drain, reserving the cooking water.

3. Purée

 15 mins

Depending on the tastes and teething stage of your baby, you don't have to purée foods as finely at this stage (you can even just mash some vegetables with a spoon).

VEAL + all its vegetables

SOLE Check that it doesn't contain any bones, and remove them carefully if it does. Purée with its cooking juices + half the chervil + a little water or vegetable cooking water if necessary.

CARROT AND TURNIP + half the coriander + 30 g (1 oz) fromage frais

POTATO + 10 g (¼ oz) butter: put through a food mill or mash with a fork (avoid using a blender)

ASPARAGUS AND HALF THE PEAS + 1 teaspoon olive oil + 4–5 mint leaves

REST OF THE PEAS +10 g (¼ oz) butter

ZUCCHINI + 2 teaspoons olive oil + the rest of the coriander and chervil

TOMATOES (tinned) + 1 tablespoon olive oil

LENTILS + 1 teaspoon olive oil

FRUIT Purée the apples, strawberries (set aside a few whole ones) and rhubarb separately.

4. Extra preparation

FISH CAKES Take 50 g (1¾ oz) sole + 50 g (1¾ oz) mashed potato. Shape into 6 balls and flatten them slightly. Brown them for 2–3 minutes on each side in a frying pan with 2 teaspoons oil.

FLANS Purée together 1 egg + 300 g (10½ oz) herbed zucchini + 30 g (1 oz) grated parmesan cheese + 50 ml (1½ fl oz) milk. Pour into two buttered ramekins or silicone moulds. Steam for 20 minutes or bake for 20 minutes at 160°C (320°F). Unmould.

5. Weigh

 15 mins

Weigh out the purées for the week and put them into containers.

MONDAY ➜ 200 g (7 oz) veal navarin
➜ 100 g (3½ oz) apple
➜ 100 g (3½ oz) asparagus and peas

TUESDAY ➜ 3 fish cakes + 100 g (3½ oz) zucchini
➜ 200 g (7 oz) apple and rhubarb*
➜ 100 g (3½ oz) tomato

WEDNESDAY ➜ zucchini flan
➜ 100 g (3½ oz) carrot and turnip with coriander and fromage frais

THURSDAY ➜ 150 g (5½ oz) veal navarin + 50 g (1¾ oz) potato
➜ 100 g (3½ oz) strawberries
➜ 100 g (3½ oz) peas + 2 tablespoons yoghurt

FRIDAY ➜ 15 g (½ oz) sole + 200 g (7 oz) zucchini
➜ 50 g (1¾ oz) apple + 50 g (1¾ oz) strawberry
➜ 50 g (1¾ oz) lentils + 20 g (¾ oz) tomato + 30 g (1 oz) zucchini

BONUS RECIPE ➜ 30 g (1 oz) each apple + strawberry

LUNCHTIME DESSERTS ➜ 100 g (3½ oz) apple
➜ 50 g (1¾ oz) rhubarb + 50 g (1¾ oz) strawberry

*This large container contains several serves of apple and rhubarb purée – it should be enough for at least two meals. If you prefer, you can divide into 100 g (3½ oz) portions (= 1 meal) in 150 ml (5½ fl oz) containers.

6. Store

STORING Clearly label ➜ Monday's portions in the refrigerator and other portions in the freezer.

LEFTOVERS Freeze any extras in ice cube trays to make 10–20 g (¼–¾ oz) portions. For the sole and veal, weigh out 15 g (½ oz) portions. ➜ **FREEZER**

Veal navarin / Apple purée with yoghurt / Asparagus and pea risotto

🕐 Ready in 10 minutes (25 minutes for dinner)

LUNCH Reheat the veal navarin. Offer small pieces of strawberry (or purée them) for dessert.

SNACK Serve the apple purée with a yoghurt.

DINNER Heat 500 ml (17 fl oz) water with ½ stock cube crumbled into it. Peel and finely chop the shallot, sweat it for 5 minutes over low heat in 1 teaspoon butter, add 20 g (¾ oz) rice and stir until translucent. Gradually add the stock, stirring, until the rice is very tender (about 20 minutes). Add ½ teaspoon crème fraîche and 10 g (¼ oz) grated parmesan cheese. Reheat the asparagus and pea purée and mix it into the rice.

Sole fish cakes / Apple and rhubarb mousse / Pasta and tomato sauce

🕐 Ready in 10 minutes (25 minutes for dinner)

LUNCH Reheat the fish cakes with the zucchini purée. Offer pieces of banana for dessert.
SNACK Process 70–100 g (2½–3½ oz) yoghurt with 100 g (3½ oz) apple and rhubarb purée.
DINNER Cook 30 g (1 oz) pasta. Serve with the tomato purée, a small knob of butter and 10 g (¼ oz) grated parmesan cheese. Make the rice pudding for the next day: heat 200 ml (7 fl oz) milk with ½ vanilla bean split in half. Pour in 20 g (¾ oz) rice in a stream, stir and cook over low heat for about 20 minutes, stirring as much as possible. You can sweeten it slightly with sugar.

Zucchini and parmesan flan / Rice pudding /
Carrot and coriander soup with fromage frais

🕐 Ready in 10 mins

LUNCH Place a zucchini and parmesan flan in a bowl and reheat it in a double boiler. Offer some rhubarb and strawberry purée for dessert.
SNACK Offer a portion of the rice pudding made the night before.
DINNER Reheat the carrot, turnip and coriander purée and add some water to make a soup-like consistency.

Veal and mashed potato / Strawberry smoothie / Pasta with peas

🕐 Ready in 10 mins

LUNCH Reheat the veal navarin and mashed potato. Offer an apple and rhubarb purée for dessert.

SNACK Purée the portion of strawberry with 2–3 tablespoons yoghurt and thin out with a little milk to make a smoothie.

DINNER Reheat the pea purée. Cook 30 g (1 oz) pasta. Mix together, thinning out the pea purée to make a sauce. Add 20 g (¾ oz) fromage frais and about 10 g (¼ oz) grated parmesan cheese.

Sole with chervil and zucchini / Rice pudding with apple and strawberry purée / Green lentil and zucchini soup

🕐 Ready in 10 mins

LUNCH Reheat the sole and zucchini purée. Offer a simple apple purée for dessert.
SNACK Offer the rest of the rice pudding with a little apple and strawberry purée to flavour it.
DINNER Reheat the lentils, tomto and zucchini purées and add some water to make a soup-like consistency.

Muffins
(for babies who can already chew)

🕐 Ready in 20 mins

Preheat the oven to 180°C (350°F). Melt 10 g (¼ oz) butter and allow to cool. Mix 40 g (1½ oz) plain flour and a pinch of baking powder with 1 teaspoon sugar. Add the 60 g (2¼ oz) portion of apple and strawberry purée and mix well. Pour into small muffin moulds and cook for about 10–15 minutes.

Meal plans 12 months +

sample week n°1

Timing

2 HRS IN THE KITCHEN

Season: spring

In other seasons, replace the pumpkin with carrots.

Daily requirements*

Meat or fish: 20–25 g (¾–1 oz) at lunchtime

Vegetables: 200–500 g (7 oz–1 lb 2 oz)

Fruit: 3–4 serves a day, alternating fresh fruit and purées

Milk and dairy products: 500–800 ml (17–28 fl oz)

Starchy foods: 75–100 g (2½–3½ oz) – cooked weight – in the evening

*Check the recommendations of your paediatrician.

Monday

Fish pie
Semolina pudding
Pasta with pumpkin and broccoli

Tuesday

Rice and meatballs in tomato sauce
Banana smoothie
Pumpkin and sweet potato soup with cheese

Wednesday

Egg-in-a-nest
Baked custard
Pasta and tomato sauce

Thursday

Fish pie
Mango smoothie
Rice with broccoli

Friday

Couscous with meatballs in tomato sauce
Fruit mousse
Pumpkin and sweet potato soup with garlic bread

bonus recipe

Swiss roll

For storing

12 x 250–300 ml (9–10½ fl oz) containers

3 x 150–200 ml (5½–7 fl oz) containers

Equipment

1 steamer

1 cast-iron pot or saucepan

1 frying pan

1 blender or food processor for puréeing

2 ramekins

1 ovenproof dish

1 baking tray, 40 x 30 cm (16 x 12 inches)

shopping list

Fruit, vegetables and herbs

- ❏ 500 g (1 lb 2 oz) potatoes
- ❏ 400 g (14 oz) butternut pumpkin
- ❏ 400 g (14 oz) broccoli
- ❏ 1 leek
- ❏ 3 onions
- ❏ 500 g (1 lb 2 oz) sweet potato
- ❏ 1 sprig thyme
- ❏ 2 garlic cloves
- ❏ 5–6 sprigs basil
- ❏ 2 lemons
- ❏ 1 kg (2 lb 4 oz) apples
- ❏ 1 kg (2 lb 4 oz) pears
- ❏ 1 banana
- ❏ 40 g (1½ oz) frozen mango
- ❏ 300 g (10½ oz) frozen raspberries
- ❏ fresh fruit for each day

Refrigerated

- ❏ 50 g (1¾ oz) minced beef
- ❏ 4 eggs
- ❏ 40 g (1½ oz) parmesan cheese
- ❏ 50 g (1¾ oz) sea bream fillet or other white fish
- ❏ 30 g (1 oz) crème fraîche
- ❏ 20 g (¾ oz) butter
- ❏ 40 g (1½ oz) emmental or cheddar cheese
- ❏ 1 litre (35 fl oz) milk
- ❏ 4 small tubs yoghurt + 1–2 serves dairy per day (adapt to the advice of your paediatrician and your baby's tastes)

Groceries

- ❏ 400 g (14 oz) tin tomatoes
- ❏ 40–60 g (1½–2¼ oz) long-grain rice
- ❏ 60–80 g (2¼–2¾ oz) small pasta shapes
- ❏ 2 teaspoons baking powder
- ❏ 150 g (5½ oz) plain flour
- ❏ ½ teaspoon tahini or almond butter (optional)
- ❏ 20 g (¾ oz) fine semolina
- ❏ 30 g (1 oz) couscous
- ❏ 1 organic salt-free vegetable stock cube
- ❏ a few drops of orange flower water
- ❏ ½ vanilla bean

In the cupboard

- ❏ olive or canola oil
- ❏ ground cinnamon
- ❏ nutmeg
- ❏ 125 g (4½ oz) sugar

Sunday

1. Prepare

🕐 20 mins

■ Wash the vegetables. Peel and cut the potatoes, sweet potato and butternut pumpkin into cubes (after removing the seeds). Cut the broccoli into small florets. Trim the ends of the leek, split it in half lengthways almost all the way down and rinse it well, then thinly slice.
■ Peel and finely chop the onions. Peel and grate 1 garlic clove (save the other for during the week). Set aside 2 teaspoons chopped onion and ½ teaspoon garlic for the meatballs.
■ Rinse and dry the thyme and basil, and pick the leaves.
■ Wash and peel the apples and pears, then remove the cores and cut them into slices.

2. Fruit

🕐 15 mins

Cook the apples for 10–15 minutes, covered, over medium heat, with 1 tablespoon of water + 1 pinch cinnamon; cook the pears in the same way + ½ vanilla bean, split in two, instead of the cinnamon. Purée, mash or leave as is depending on the tastes, development and teeth of your baby ➜ **2 X 200 G (7 OZ) CONTAINERS APPLE + 1 X 200 G (7 OZ) CONTAINER PEAR + 2 X 200 G (7 OZ) CONTAINERS PEAR AND APPLE.** These large containers of cooked fruit are for 2 meals. **(DESSERTS FOR LUNCH AND DINNER)**

3. Pumpkin and soup

🕐 20 mins

PUMPKIN Put half the onion in a cast-iron pot over medium heat with 2 teaspoons olive oil. Sauté for 7–8 minutes, add the cubes of pumpkin and stir until browned. Reduce the heat and cook, covered, for 10 minutes or until tender.
➜ **1 X 100 G (3½ OZ) CONTAINER** (broccoli will be added later), **LEAVE THE REST IN THE POT**
SOUP Add half the sweet potato and the leek to the pot and stir. Add water to just cover the vegetables and crumble in ½ stock cube. Cook, covered, for about 20 minutes.
Purée ➜ **2 X 200 G (7 OZ) CONTAINERS (TUESDAY DINNER + FRIDAY DINNER)**

4. Steamed vegetables

 10 mins

Steam the vegetables (they can be cooked together, but don't mix them together, so you can take them out separately) or simmer them: the broccoli for 15 minutes, the potatoes and sweet potato for 30–35 minutes (adjust the cooking time to the steamer: the vegetables need to be tender). Save the cooking water.

5. Meatballs in tomato sauce

 25 mins

TOMATO SAUCE In a saucepan or cast-iron pot, sweat the other half of the onion for 7–8 minutes in 2 teaspoons olive oil. Add the grated garlic, stir for 1 minute. Add the tomatoes and 4–5 basil leaves and simmer for 15 minutes. Purée ➔ **1 X 125 G (4½ OZ) CONTAINER (WEDNESDAY DINNER) + THE REST IN A BOWL** (for the meatballs)
MEATBALLS Combine the minced beef + 50 g (1¾ oz) cooked and mashed potato + the reserved garlic and onion + 4–5 chopped basil leaves + the thyme. Shape into balls. Brown them in a frying pan in 2 teaspoons oil, then add the rest of the tomato sauce and simmer, covered, for 15 minutes over low heat. ➔ **DIVIDE INTO 2 CONTAINERS (TUESDAY LUNCH + FRIDAY LUNCH)**

6. Fish pie with broccoli

 20 mins

FISH PIE Preheat the oven to 180°C (350°F). Divide the bream between two ramekins. Top with 100 g (3½ oz) cooked broccoli, 1 tablespoon crème fraîche, a few drops lemon juice and 4–5 chopped basil leaves. Roughly mash 150 g (5½ oz) sweet potato and 150 g (5½ oz) potato with 10 g (¼ oz) butter, 3 tablespoons milk and a tiny pinch of salt and nutmeg. Spoon the mixture over the fish. Cook for 20–25 minutes: the fish must be cooked through. Allow to cool. ➔ **COVER WITH PLASTIC WRAP OR PLACE INTO 2 BAGS (MONDAY LUNCH + THURSDAY LUNCH)**
BROCCOLI Roughly purée the rest of the broccoli, adding a little cooking water. ➔ **1 X 100 G (3½ OZ) CONTAINER (THURSDAY DINNER) + ADD 50 G (1¾ OZ) TO THE 100 G (3½ OZ) CONTAINER OF PUMPKIN (MONDAY DINNER)**
  Combine the rest of the broccoli with the rest of the cooked and mashed potato + 10 g (¼ oz) butter + 3 tablespoons milk. ➔ **1 X 200 G (7 OZ) CONTAINER (WEDNESDAY LUNCH)**

7. Store

 5 mins

STORING Clearly label ➔ Monday's portions in the refrigerator and other portions in the freezer. Set aside some basil leaves for during the week (in a bag or container). ➔ **REFRIGERATOR**
LEFTOVERS Freeze any extras in ice cube trays.

Fish pie / Semolina pudding / Pasta with pumpkin and broccoli

Ready in 10 minutes (20 minutes for dinner)

LUNCH Reheat the fish pie.

SNACK Heat 200 ml (7 fl oz) milk with a few drops of orange flower water. Pour in 20 g (¾ oz) fine semolina in a stream and cook gently, stirring, until the mixture is thick. It can be lightly sweetened with a little sugar or jam.

DINNER Cook 30–40 g (1–1½ oz) pasta. Heat the portion of pumpkin and broccoli in a frying pan. Add a little crème fraîche and 20 g (¾ oz) grated parmesan cheese and mix with the pasta.

Rice and meatballs in tomato sauce / Banana smoothie / Pumpkin and sweet potato soup with cheese

🕐 Ready in 10 minutes (15 minutes for lunch)

LUNCH Cook 20–30 g (¾–1 oz) rice. Reheat the meatballs in tomato sauce and serve with the rice and some chopped basil.

SNACK Purée 70–100 g (2½–3½ oz) yoghurt with ½ banana and some milk to thin it out.

DINNER Reheat the soup, serve with 20 g (¾ oz) cubed emmental or cheddar cheese and some bread.

FOR WEDNESDAY Make the baked custard (2–3 ramekins). Preheat the oven to 160°C (320°F). Whisk 1 egg with 1 tablespoon sugar. Heat 200 ml (7 fl oz) milk, whisk it into the mixture, pour into ramekins and place in an ovenproof dish. Pour water into the dish to reach halfway up the sides of the ramekins and cook for 20–25 minutes. Cool, then refrigerate (48 hours maximum).

Egg-in-a-nest / Baked custard / Pasta and tomato sauce

🕐 Ready in 10 mins

LUNCH Reheat the mashed potato with broccoli in a small frying pan with a little milk, stirring. Make a hole in the middle and break in an egg. Cook until the white is well cooked and the yolk is still a little runny.
SNACK Serve a baked custard.
DINNER Cook 30–40 g (1–1½ oz) pasta. Serve it with the tomato sauce and a little grated parmesan.

Fish pie / Mango smoothie / Rice with broccoli

Ready in 10 mins

LUNCH Reheat the fish pie.

SNACK Purée the thawed mango with some milk and about 50 g (1¾ oz) yoghurt (save the rest of the tub for dinner).

DINNER Put 20–30 g (¾–1 oz) rice in a saucepan with one and a half times its volume of water. Bring to the boil, cover and cook for 11 minutes. Reheat the broccoli, mix with the rice, 1 tablespoon yoghurt, ½ teaspoon almond butter or tahini, a few drops of lemon juice and ½ teaspoon olive oil.

FOR FRIDAY Buy some bread.

Couscous with meatballs in tomato sauce / Fruit mousse / Pumpkin and sweet potato soup with garlic bread

🕐 Ready in 15 mins

LUNCH Reheat the meatballs. Cook 30 g (1 oz) couscous by pouring over the same volume of boiling water, covering and waiting for 5 minutes (or follow the instructions on the packet). Serve with the meatballs.
SNACK Purée some cooked fruit with some yoghurt to make a fruit mousse.
DINNER Reheat the pumpkin and sweet potato purée and add some water to make a soup-like consistency. Serve with some bread rubbed with garlic and topped with grated emmental or cheddar cheese.

Swiss roll

🕐 Ready in 1 hour 30 mins

Preheat the oven to 190°C (375°F). Whisk 2 eggs with 120 g (4¼ oz) sugar until the mixture is pale and airy.
Add 150 g (5½ oz) plain flour mixed with 2 teaspoons baking powder, stir, then add 500 ml (17 fl oz) milk
and whisk just until the batter is smooth. Pour into a shallow rectangular baking tray lined with baking paper.
Bake for 8–10 minutes, then lift out the cake using the baking paper. Spread 300 g (10s oz) thawed raspberries
mixed with a little thick yoghurt and sugar over the cake and roll up. Chill for at least 1 hour before serving.

Meal plans 12 months +

sample week n°2

Timing
2 HRS
IN THE KITCHEN

Season: winter

In other seasons, replace the cauliflower with broccoli or zucchini (courgette).

Daily requirements*

Meat or fish: 20–25 g (¾–1 oz) at lunchtime

Vegetables: 200–500 g (7 oz–1 lb 2 oz)

Fruit: 3–4 serves a day, alternating fresh fruit and purées

Milk and dairy products: 500–800 ml (17–28 fl oz)

Starchy foods: 75–100 g (2½–3½ oz) – cooked weight – in the evening

*Check the recommendations of your paediatrician.

Monday
Orange fish parcel and vegetables
Semolina pudding
Pasta and tomato sauce

Tuesday
Lamb tagine
Banana on bread
Leek and potato soup with cream and chives

Wednesday
Red lentil soup
Porridge
Fried rice with egg

Thursday
Mashed potato and ham
Hot chocolate
Red lentil soup

Friday
Lamb tagine
Banana smoothie
Leek and potato soup

bonus recipe
Yoghurt cake

For storing

13 x 250–300 ml (9–10½ fl oz) containers

3 x 150–200 ml (5½–7 fl oz) containers

Equipment

1 steamer

2 cast-iron pots or saucepans

1 frying pan

1 blender or food processor for puréeing

Baking paper

1 cake tin

shopping list

Fruit, vegetables and herbs

- ❏ 500 g (1 lb 2 oz) potatoes
- ❏ 400 g (14 oz) carrots
- ❏ 400 g (14 oz) cauliflower
- ❏ 4 leeks
- ❏ 10–12 chives
- ❏ 3 small onions
- ❏ 5–6 sprigs flat-leaf parsley
- ❏ 3 garlic cloves
- ❏ a small piece fresh ginger
- ❏ 2 bananas
- ❏ 2 organic or untreated oranges
- ❏ 1 kg (2 lb 4 oz) apples
- ❏ 1 lime
- ❏ 1 kg (2 lb 4 oz) pears
- ❏ fresh fruit for each day (clementines, some kiwifruit just to taste, pears, blackberries, oranges, mango, pineapple...)

Refrigerated

- ❏ 20–30 g (¾–1 oz) ham
- ❏ 20–30 g (¾–1 oz) cod fillet
- ❏ 50 g (1¾ oz) piece of lamb leg or shoulder, cut into pieces
- ❏ 20 g (¾ oz) parmesan cheese or other grating cheese
- ❏ 2 small tubs yoghurt + 1–2 serves dairy per day (adapt to the advice of your paediatrician and your baby's tastes)
- ❏ 3 eggs
- ❏ 10 g (¼ oz) crème fraîche
- ❏ 20 g (¾ oz) emmental or cheddar cheese
- ❏ 25 g (1 oz) butter
- ❏ 500 ml (17 fl oz) milk

Groceries

- ❏ 1 organic salt-free vegetable stock cube
- ❏ ½ vanilla bean
- ❏ 10 dried apricots
- ❏ 20 g (¾ oz) red lentils
- ❏ 400 g (14 oz) tin tomatoes
- ❏ 1 teaspoon baking powder
- ❏ 30–40 g (1–1½ oz) small pasta shapes
- ❏ 180 g (6 oz) plain flour
- ❏ 90 ml (3 fl oz) coconut milk
- ❏ 20 g (¾ oz) fine semolina
- ❏ 50 g (1¾ oz) couscous or burghul
- ❏ 40 g (1½ oz) long-grain rice
- ❏ a few drops of orange flower water
- ❏ 20 g (¾ oz) rolled oats
- ❏ 1 slice wholemeal bread
- ❏ 10–15 g (¼–½ oz) dark chocolate

In the cupboard

- ❏ olive oil and canola oil (or other neutral-flavoured oil)
- ❏ honey (optional)
- ❏ 100 g (3½ oz) sugar
- ❏ ground cumin
- ❏ nutmeg
- ❏ ground cinnamon
- ❏ salt

week n°2 Sunday

1. Prepare

🕐 20 mins

■ Wash the vegetables. Peel the potatoes and carrots. Dice the potatoes and slice the carrots into rounds. Cut the cauliflower into small florets. Trim the green ends of the leeks, split them in half down most of the length to thoroughly rinse out any dirt and then slice them thinly.

■ Peel the onions and finely chop two of them; thinly slice the third onion. Peel the garlic cloves and grate one of them.

■ Rinse and dry the parsley sprigs, then pick the parsley leaves.

■ Wash and peel the apples and pears, remove the cores and cut them into slices.

2. Fruit

🕐 15 mins

Cook each of the fruits separately for 10–15 minutes, covered, over medium heat, with 1 tablespoon of water: the apples + 1 pinch cinnamon and 5 chopped dried apricots; the pears + ½ vanilla bean, split down the middle. Purée, mash or leave as is depending on the tastes, development and teeth of your baby. ➔ **2 X 200 G (7 OZ) CONTAINERS OF PEAR** Juice ½ orange and add it to the apple and apricot. ➔ **3 X 200 G (7 OZ) CONTAINERS OF APPLE AND APRICOT (DESSERTS LUNCH/EVENING)**

3. Tomato sauce

🕐 15 mins

In a saucepan or cast-iron pot, sweat the chopped onions for 7–8 minutes in 2 teaspoons olive oil. ➔ **HALF IN A BOWL.** Add half a grated garlic clove, stir 1 minute, add 200 g (7 oz) tinned tomatoes and around 10 parsley leaves and simmer for 15 minutes. Purée. ➔ **I X 125 G (4½ OZ) CONTAINER (MONDAY DINNER)**

4. Soup and purée

🕐 20 mins

LEEK AND POTATO SOUP Put the cooked onions you've set aside in another pot with the potatoes, ½ crumbled stock cube and water to cover. Cook, covered, for about 15–20 minutes until tender ➔ **HALF IN A BOWL** (use a slotted spoon to remove). Add the leeks and cook for about 10 minutes. Put through a food mill (or leave the pieces whole, but avoid blending so the potato doesn't become gluey). ➔ **2 X 200 G (7 OZ) CONTAINERS (TUESDAY DINNER + FRIDAY DINNER) PURÉE** Mash the rest of the potatoes + 15 g (½ oz) butter + 50 ml (1½ fl oz) milk ➔ **I X 200 G (7 OZ) CONTAINER (THURSDAY LUNCH)**

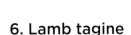

5. Lentil soup

 10 mins

Rinse the red lentils, put them in a saucepan with 100 g (3½ oz) tinned tomatoes, half the ginger, 1 garlic clove, the sliced onion, 1 pinch cumin and 1 pinch cinnamon. Cover with water and cook for 15 minutes (the lentils will fall apart). Purée in a blender or food processor with 3 tablespoons coconut milk.
→ **2 X 200 G (7 OZ) CONTAINERS (WEDNESDAY LUNCH + THURSDAY DINNER)**

6. Lamb tagine

 20 mins

Brown the lamb pieces in 1 tablespoon olive oil over medium–high heat. Lower the heat, add 1 garlic clove and 1 large pinch grated ginger (save a little for vegetables with the rice). Cook, stirring, for 1 minute, add 1 good pinch of cumin and 1 good pinch of cinnamon and stir well for 1 minute. Add 200 g (7 oz) carrots, 5 chopped apricots, ½ crumbled stock cube, the rest of the tomatoes and enough water to half cover the ingredients. Cover and simmer for 30 minutes over very low heat. →
DIVIDE INTO 2 CONTAINERS (TUESDAY LUNCH + FRIDAY LUNCH)

7. Steamed vegetables, fish and rice

 15 mins

STEAMED VEGETABLES Steam the vegetables (they can be cooked together, but don't mix them up so you can take them out separately) or simmer: cauliflower for 15 minutes, carrots for 25 minutes (adjust the cooking time to the steamer: the vegetables need to be tender). → **2 CONTAINERS OF 50 G (1¾ OZ) CARROT + 50 G (1¾ OZ) CAULIFLOWER (MONDAY LUNCH + WEDNESDAY DINNER).** Add 1 pinch grated ginger + 1 pinch garlic to the Wednesday container and mix.
FISH Lay the fish on some baking paper, add 1 teaspoon olive oil, 1 slice orange, 5–6 small parsley leaves and a tiny pinch of salt. Seal the parcel (it will be cooked Monday lunch). → **REFRIGERATOR**
RICE Cook the rice for 11 minutes in lightly salted boiling water, then drain.
→ **1 CONTAINER (WEDNESDAY DINNER)**

8. Store

 5 mins

STORING Clearly label → Monday's portions in the refrigerator and other portions in the freezer.
Set aside a few parsley leaves and the chives for during the week (in a bag or container). →**REFRIGERATOR**
LEFTOVERS Freeze any extras in ice cube trays or in bags if the vegetables are in pieces.

Monday

Orange fish parcel and vegetables /
Semolina pudding / Pasta and tomato sauce

🕐 Ready in 10 minutes (15 minutes for lunch)

LUNCH Preheat the oven to 200°C (400°F). Cook the parcel for 10–15 minutes. Reheat the container of cauliflower and carrots and serve with the fish.

SNACK Heat 200 ml (7 fl oz) milk with a few drops of orange flower water. Pour in 20 g (¾ oz) fine semolina in a stream. Cook gently, stirring, until the mixture is thick. It can be lightly sweetened with a little sugar or jam.

DINNER Cook 30–40 g (1–1½ oz) pasta. Reheat the tomato sauce and add 1 teaspoon butter. Serve with some grated parmesan cheese.

Lamb tagine / Banana on bread /
Leek and potato soup with cream and chives

Ready in 10 mins

LUNCH Cook 25 g (1 oz) couscous or burghul according to the packet instructions (this varies depending on the type of couscous). Reheat the lamb tagine and serve with the couscous, sprinkling with chopped parsley.

SNACK Butter a slice of bread (preferably wholemeal). Place a row of banana slices on top and sprinkle with a little ground cinnamon.

DINNER Reheat the soup and serve with a dollop of crème fraîche and chopped chives (keep some aside for Friday).

Wednesday

Red lentil soup / Porridge / Fried rice with egg

Ready in 10 mins

LUNCH Reheat the lentil soup and add a few drops of lime juice (save some for the next day).
SNACK Heat 150 ml (5 fl oz) milk, add 20 g (¾ oz) rolled oats in a stream and cook for a few minutes, stirring. Sweeten with a little cooked fruit or honey.
DINNER Heat 2 teaspoons oil in a hot frying pan, break in an egg and stir vigorously to cook. Add the container of carrots and cauliflower with ginger and garlic and stir for 2 minutes. Add the container of rice, stir for 1 minute. Add 30 ml (1 fl oz) coconut milk and cook for another 2–3 minutes.

Mashed potato and ham / Hot chocolate / Red lentil soup

🕐 Ready in 10 mins

LUNCH Reheat the mashed potato (in a double boiler or a saucepan with a little milk). Serve with the chopped ham.
SNACK Heat 200 ml (7 fl oz) milk. Break up the chocolate, add it to the milk and whisk until it's completely melted. Serve (not too hot) with a small plain biscuit. You can flavour it with some vanilla or a pinch of cinnamon.
DINNER Reheat the lentil soup and serve with a few drops of lime (thin it out a little with water if necessary).

Lamb tagine / Banana smoothie / Leek and potato soup
🕐 Ready in 15 mins

LUNCH Cook 25 g (1 oz) burghul or couscous. Reheat the lamb tagine.
SNACK Purée a banana with some yoghurt and some milk to thin it out.
DINNER Reheat the soup and serve with chopped chives and cubes of emmental or cheddar cheese.

Yoghurt cake

🕐 Ready in 40 mins

Preheat the oven to 180°C (350°F). Empty a small tub of yoghurt into a mixing bowl. Add 1½ yoghurt tubs of sugar, 2 eggs and a little orange zest, and whisk together. Add ½ yoghurt tub of neutral-flavoured oil and whisk together. Add 3 yoghurt tubs of plain flour + 1 teaspoon baking powder and a tiny pinch of salt. Mix together and pour into a buttered cake tin. Cook for 30 minutes.

Meal plans 12 months +

Timing

2 HRS
IN THE KITCHEN

Season: winter

In other seasons, replace the strawberries with frozen raspberries and the asparagus with broad beans.

Daily requirements*

Meat or fish: 20–25 g (¾–1 oz) at lunchtime

Vegetables: 200–500 g (7 oz–1 lb 2 oz)

Fruit: 3–4 serves a day, alternating fresh fruit and purées

Milk and dairy products: 500–800 ml (17–28 fl oz)

Starchy foods: 75–100 g (2½–3½ oz) – cooked weight – in the evening

*Check the recommendations of your paediatrician.

Monday
Salmon and spinach lasagne
Strawberries and cream
Spinach and zucchini soup

Tuesday
Veal involtini with herbs
Mini bircher muesli
Vegetable fritters

Wednesday
Egg and asparagus
Strawberry and banana smoothie
Pasta and green sauce

Thursday
Salmon and spinach lasagne
Semolina pudding
Vegetable fritters

Friday
Veal involtini with herbs
Chocolate yoghurt
Spinach and zucchini soup

bonus recipe
Mini trifle

For storing

11 x 250–300 ml (9–10½ fl oz) containers

2 x 150–200 ml (5½–7 fl oz) containers

3 or 4 freezer bags

Equipment

1 steamer

1 cast-iron pot or saucepan

1 frying pan

1 blender or food processor for puréeing

2 ramekins

1–2 wooden toothpicks

shopping list

Fruit, vegetables and herbs

- ❏ 1 carrot
- ❏ 600 g (1 lb 5 oz) zucchini (courgettes)
- ❏ 500 g (1 lb 2 oz) frozen spinach
- ❏ 200 g (7 oz) peas
- ❏ 100 g (3½ oz) frozen or shelled broad beans
- ❏ 100 g (3½ oz) snow peas
- ❏ 8 thin asparagus spears
- ❏ 2 onions
- ❏ 2 garlic cloves
- ❏ 5–6 sprigs flat-leaf parsley
- ❏ 3–4 sage leaves
- ❏ 5–6 sprigs chervil or flat-leaf parsley
- ❏ 500 g (1 lb 2 oz) rhubarb
- ❏ 2 organic or untreated lemons
- ❏ 500 g (1 lb 2 oz) strawberries + 200 g (7 oz) for bonus recipe
- ❏ 700 g (1 lb 9 oz) apples
- ❏ 1 orange
- ❏ 1 banana
- ❏ fresh fruit for each day

Refrigerated

- ❏ 50 g (1¾ oz) wild salmon fillet
- ❏ 50 g (1¾ oz) veal steak
- ❏ 1 slice prosciutto
- ❏ 180 g (6 oz) ricotta cheese
- ❏ 3 eggs
- ❏ 600 ml (21 fl oz) milk
- ❏ 20 g (¾ oz) emmental or cheddar cheese
- ❏ 40 g (1½ oz) parmesan cheese
- ❏ 3 small tubs yoghurt + 1–2 serves of dairy per day (adapt to the advice of your paediatrician and your baby's tastes)
- ❏ 150 ml (5 fl oz) pouring cream
- ❏ 25 g (1 oz) butter

Groceries

- ❑ 2–3 lasagne sheets
- ❑ 10 g (¼ oz) cornflour
- ❑ 20 g (¾ oz) fine semolina
- ❑ 100 g (3½ oz) plain flour
- ❑ 15 g (½ oz) baby oat flakes
- ❑ 1 organic salt-free vegetable stock cube
- ❑ a few drops of orange flower water
- ❑ 1 medjool date (or other dried fruit)
- ❑ ½ teaspoon cocoa powder
- ❑ 30–40 g (1–1½ oz) small pasta shapes
- ❑ 5 sponge finger biscuits

In the cupboard

- ❑ olive or canola oil
- ❑ 80 g (2¾ oz) sugar
- ❑ ground cinnamon
- ❑ honey (optional)

1. Prepare

🕐 20 mins

- Wash the vegetables and peel the carrot. Slice all the zucchini except 1 into rounds and the snow peas into strips. Trim the tough ends of the asparagus spears.
- Peel and finely chop the onions. Peel and grate 1 garlic clove (save the other for during the week). Rinse and dry the parsley, chervil and sage, and pick the leaves.
- Wash the rhubarb and cut into short lengths.
- Wash and hull the strawberries. Keep about 150 g (5½ oz) of them whole.
- Peel and core the apples, and cut into slices.

2. Fruit

🕐 15 mins

Cook, covered, over medium heat: apples + 1 tablespoon water + 1 pinch cinnamon, for 10–15 minutes; rhubarb + 3 tablespoons water + 60 g (2¼ oz) sugar, for 15 minutes. Purée, mash or leave as is depending on the tastes, development and teeth of your baby. ➜ **2 X 200 G (7 OZ) CONTAINERS OF APPLE AND RHUBARB.**

Purée 350 g (12 oz) strawberries with a little lemon juice and a little sugar.
➜ **1 X 200 G (7 OZ) CONTAINER OF STRAWBERRIES + 2 X 200 G (7 OZ) CONTAINERS OF APPLE AND STRAWBERRY (DESSERTS FOR LUNCH / EVENING)**

3. Soup

🕐 15 mins

Sweat the onion for 7–8 minutes in 2 teaspoons olive oil in a saucepan or cast-iron pot.

➜ **HALF IN A BOWL.** Add the grated garlic, stir for 1 minute, then add 300 g (10½ oz) zucchini rounds, ½ crumbled stock cube and enough water to barely cover the zucchini. Cook for 15 minutes. Add 200 g (7 oz) spinach, 10 leaves parsley and 2 sprigs chervil, and cook for 10 minutes. Set aside a ladleful of the cooking liquid. Purée.
➜ **2 X 200 G (7 OZ) CONTAINERS (MONDAY DINNER + FRIDAY DINNER)**

4. Lasagne

 20 mins

Preheat the oven to 180°C (350°F). Finely chop the rest of the parsley and chervil by hand or in a food processor. Mix with 65–80 g (2¼–2¾ oz) ricotta. Divide into two portions (half for the lasagne, half for the veal).

Steam the spinach for 5–10 minutes. → **200 G (7 OZ) FOR THE LASAGNE, THE REST FOR THE VEGETABLES.** Chop the salmon. In two buttered ramekins, make a layer of salmon, a layer of ricotta, a layer of lasagne (depending on the size of the ramekins, cut each lasagne sheet into two or three pieces), a layer of spinach, a few peas, then repeat. Add 1–2 teaspoons cream to each ramekin and moisten with the reserved cooking liquid. Cook for 30 minutes, then allow to cool. → **FREEZER BAG (MONDAY LUNCH + THURSDAY LUNCH)**

5. Veal

 20 mins

If the veal is thick, place a sheet of baking paper on top and gently flatten the veal with a rolling pin. Spread the ricotta mixture, the slice of prosciutto and the chopped sage leaves over the veal, then roll up. Use a small toothpick to hold the roll together. Steam for about 15–20 minutes. Cut in half. Remove the toothpick. → **PLACE EACH HALF IN THE BOTTOM OF TWO LARGE CONTAINERS**

6. Fritters

 10 mins

Grate the carrot and reserved zucchini.
→ **FREEZER BAG (TUESDAY DINNER)**

7. Vegetables

 15 mins

Return the bowl of reserved onion to the pot. Add 2 asparagus spears, the peas, broad beans, snow peas and the rest of the zucchini. Add 100 ml (3½ fl oz) water and ½ crumbled stock cube and cook for 5–10 minutes until everything is *al dente*. Add the (already cooked) spinach. Purée 150 g (5½ oz) of the mixture + 1 tablespoon olive oil until smooth. This will be the sauce for the pasta. → **1 CONTAINER (WEDNESDAY DINNER)**

Leave the rest of the vegetables whole or roughly purée them according to your baby's preferences. → **ADD 200 G (7 OZ) VEGETABLES TO EACH CONTAINER OF VEAL (TUESDAY LUNCH + FRIDAY LUNCH)**

Mix the remaining asparagus with 1 tablespoon of olive oil, 1 pinch salt and 1 pinch lemon zest. → **FREEZER BAG (WEDNESDAY LUNCH)**

8. Store

 5 mins

STORING Clearly label → Monday's portions in the refrigerator and other portions in the freezer.
LEFTOVERS Freeze any extras in ice cube trays or in other suitable containers.

Salmon and spinach lasagne / Strawberries and cream / Spinach and zucchini soup

🕐 Ready in 10 mins

LUNCH Reheat the lasagne.
SNACK Serve some lightly sweetened strawberries with 1 teaspoon cream mixed into some yoghurt.
DINNER Reheat the soup (thinning it out if necessary). Serve with lightly buttered pieces of bread.

Veal involtini with herbs / Mini bircher muesli / Vegetable fritters

🕐 Ready in 10 mins

LUNCH Reheat the veal involtini and vegetables. Slice the involtini.

SNACK In the morning, put the oat flakes in a bowl, cover with milk and store in the refrigerator (they will become thick like a porridge). Serve with the chopped pitted date, optional fresh fruit and a pinch of cinnamon.

DINNER Whisk together 100 g (3½ oz) plain flour and 1 egg, thin out with enough milk to obtain a dropping consistency, and add the thawed grated vegetables. Cook ladlefuls of batter in a frying pan with a little butter. Serve about half of these fritters and keep the others carefully wrapped in the refrigerator for the day after next.

Egg and asparagus / Strawberry and banana smoothie / Pasta and green sauce

🕐 Ready in 15 mins

LUNCH Cook the asparagus: either simmer for 5–6 minutes in boiling water or bake for 10 minutes in a preheated 200°C (400°F) oven. Fry an egg and serve on top of the asparagus with a little grated parmesan.
SNACK Purée ½ banana with about 50 g (1¾ oz) puréed strawberry, 50 g (1¾ oz) yoghurt and milk.
DINNER Cook the pasta and serve with the green sauce, thinned out with a little of the pasta cooking water, and some grated parmesan.

Salmon and spinach lasagne / Semolina pudding / Vegetable fritters

🕐 Ready in 10 mins

LUNCH Reheat the lasagne.
SNACK Heat 200 ml (7 fl oz) milk with a few drops of orange flower water. Pour in 20 g (¾ oz) fine semolina in a stream, cook gently, stirring, until the mixture is thick. You can sweeten it with a little honey or jam.
DINNER Reheat the vegetable fritters in a lightly buttered frying pan. Serve them with yoghurt mixed with a little olive oil and a few drops of lemon juice.
FOR FRIDAY Buy some bread.

Veal involtini with herbs / Chocolate yoghurt / Spinach and zucchini soup

🕐 Ready in 15 mins

LUNCH Reheat the veal involtini and vegetables. Slice the involtini.

SNACK Beat a small tub of yoghurt with ½ teaspoon cocoa powder and ½ teaspoon of sugar (or 1 teaspoon drinking chocolate).

DINNER Reheat the soup. Serve with some bread rubbed with garlic and topped with finely grated emmental or cheddar cheese.

Mini trifle

🕐 Ready in 1 hour 30 mins

Whisk 1 egg yolk with 10 g (¼ oz) cornflour and 20 g (¾ oz) sugar. Heat 250 ml (9 fl oz) milk and pour it over the egg mixture, whisking constantly. Return to the saucepan and cook gently until it forms a thick custard. Allow to cool. Whisk 100 ml (3½ fl oz) pouring cream until firm. Mix with 100–125 g (3½–4½ oz) thick yoghurt. Dip the sponge finger biscuits in the juice of 1 orange and arrange in a large bowl. Top with 200–250 g (7–9 oz) puréed strawberries or 150 ml (5 fl oz) of your choice of fruit purée. You can also use a few cut strawberries. Cover with the custard, then the cream and yoghurt mixture. Refrigerate for at least 1 hour before serving.

Meal plans 12 months +

sample week nº4

Timing

2 HRS
IN THE KITCHEN

Season: summer

In other seasons, replace the blackberries with frozen raspberries, and the peaches and apricots with apples and pears. Use tinned peeled tomatoes.

Daily requirements*

Meat or fish: 20-25 g (¾-1 oz) at lunchtime

Vegetables: 200-500 g (7 oz-1 lb 2 oz)

Fruit: 3-4 serves a day, alternating fresh fruit and purées

Milk and dairy products: 500-800 ml (17-28 fl oz)

Starchy foods: 75-100 g (2½-3½ oz) – cooked weight – in the evening

*Check the recommendations of your paediatrician.

Monday
Tuna niçoise
Chocolate pudding
Gazpacho

Tuesday
Roast chicken and vegetables with couscous
Raspberry 'ice cream'
Pasta and creamy pesto

Wednesday
Melon salad
Banana and blackberry smoothie
Beans in tomato sauce

Thursday
Rice, chicken and summer vegetables
Strawberries on bread
Gazpacho

Friday
Tuna niçoise
Melon balls
Pasta and tomato sauce

bonus recipe
Peach charlotte

For storing

9 x 250-300 ml (9-10½ fl oz) containers

3 x 150-200 ml (5½-7 fl oz) containers

Equipment

1 steamer

1 cast-iron pot or saucepan

1 ovenproof dish

1 baking tray

1 frying pan

1 blender or food processor for puréeing

1 ramekin

1 small charlotte mould

week n°4 *shopping list*

Fruit, vegetables and herbs

- ❏ 1.2 kg (2 lb 10 oz) tomatoes
- ❏ 600 g (1 lb 5 oz) zucchini (courgettes)
- ❏ 1 small red capsicum (pepper)
- ❏ 1 eggplant (aubergine)
- ❏ 1 cucumber
- ❏ 100 g (3½ oz) cherry tomatoes
- ❏ 100 g (3½ oz) broad beans (fresh or frozen)
- ❏ 3 bulb spring onions (scallions)
- ❏ 2 garlic cloves
- ❏ 1 sprig thyme
- ❏ 1 organic or untreated lemon
- ❏ 1 sprig mint
- ❏ 1 bunch basil
- ❏ 1 lime
- ❏ 2 slices rockmelon
- ❏ 1 piece watermelon (optional)
- ❏ 1 kg (2 lb 4 oz) apricots
- ❏ 1 kg (2 lb 4 oz) peaches + 5 for the bonus recipe
- ❏ 1 banana
- ❏ 60 g (2¼ oz) frozen raspberries
- ❏ 50 g (1¾ oz) blackberries
- ❏ strawberries
- ❏ fresh fruit for each day

Refrigerated

- ☐ 50 g (1¾ oz) line-caught tuna
- ☐ 1 chicken thigh cutlet
- ☐ 300 ml (10½ fl oz) milk
- ☐ 300 g (10½ oz) ricotta cheese
- ☐ 5–6 bocconcini balls
- ☐ 15 g (½ oz) parmesan cheese or other grating cheese
- ☐ 20 g (¾ oz) butter
- ☐ 100 ml (3½ fl oz) pouring cream
- ☐ 20 g (¾ oz) emmental or cheddar cheese
- ☐ 2 small tubs yoghurt + 1–2 serves of dairy per day (adapt to the advice of your paediatrician and your baby's tastes)

Groceries

- ☐ 60–80 g (2¼–2¾ oz) small pasta shapes
- ☐ 100 g (3½ oz) tinned white beans
- ☐ 30 g (1 oz) long-grain rice
- ☐ 20 g (¾ oz) dark chocolate
- ☐ 25 g (1 oz) couscous
- ☐ 2 slices sandwich bread
- ☐ vanilla sugar (optional)
- ☐ about 15 small sponge finger biscuits

In the cupboard

- ☐ olive or canola oil
- ☐ salt
- ☐ sugar
- ☐ cornflour

Sunday

1. Prepare

🕐 20 mins

- Wash the vegetables. Cut and peel three-quarters of the cucumber (save the rest for Monday night). Slice the zucchini and cucumber into rounds and slice the capsicums (after removing the white membranes and seeds). Dice the eggplant. Peel the tomatoes: drop them into a bowl of boiling water for a few moments, then remove the skin.
- Peel the spring onions and finely chop two of them. Peel 1 garlic clove and grate or chop it. Rinse and dry the basil and thyme, then pick the leaves.
- Wash and peel the peaches, remove the stones and cut into segments.
- Wash the apricots and remove the stones.

2. Fruit

🕐 10 mins

Preheat the oven to 190°C (375°F). Place the peaches and apricots in an ovenproof dish, sprinkle with 2 teaspoons sugar, add 1–2 strips of lemon rind and cook for 35 minutes (leave the oven on for the chicken). Purée, mash or leave as is depending on the tastes, development and teeth of your baby. **→ 3 X 200 G (7 OZ) CONTAINERS (DESSERTS LUNCH / EVENING)**

3. Gazpacho

🕐 10 mins

Purée together 300 g (10½ oz) tomatoes, half the capsicum, the cucumber, 1 halved onion (the one that hasn't been chopped), 1 pinch grated garlic and 5–6 basil leaves.
→ 2 X 200 G (7 OZ) CONTAINERS (MONDAY DINNER + THURSDAY DINNER)

4. Chicken and vegetables

⏲ 20 mins

Place the chicken thigh on a baking tray, surround with zucchini slices, halved tomatoes, cubes of eggplant (don't mix the vegetables together), and the rest of the capsicum. Scatter over the onion, the grated or chopped garlic (reserve a pinch) and 10 basil leaves. Sprinkle with 2 tablespoons olive oil and a small pinch of salt. Bake for 20 minutes at 190°C (375°F), then lower the heat to 160°C (320°F) and cook for another 40 minutes, until the chicken is very tender. Remove the skin from the chicken, pull the flesh off the bones and cut into small pieces.
→ **2 CONTAINERS OF 25 G (1 OZ) CHICKEN + 150 G (5½ OZ) ZUCCHINI + 1 BAKED TOMATO (TUESDAY LUNCH + THURSDAY LUNCH)**

5. Tuna

⏲ 20 mins

Cut the tuna into pieces and brown in a frying pan in 2 teaspoons olive oil. Add 400–500 g (14 oz–1 lb 2 oz) baked vegetables (zucchini, tomatoes, capsicum and eggplant). Mix together, add a few thyme leaves and cook together for 10 minutes over very low heat. → **2 X 230 G (8 OZ) CONTAINERS (MONDAY LUNCH + FRIDAY LUNCH)**

6. Tomato coulis and pesto

⏲ 15 mins

TOMATO COULIS Purée the remaining baked tomatoes with 15 g (½ oz) butter and a tiny pinch of sugar. → **2 X 100 G (3½ OZ) CONTAINERS (WEDNESDAY DINNER + FRIDAY DINNER)**
CREAMY PESTO Cook the broad beans in 2 teaspoons olive oil and 1 tablespoon water over medium heat for 6–7 minutes. Purée the remaining basil (reserve 1 sprig) with 1 pinch garlic, 15 g (½ oz) grated parmesan, 1 tiny pinch salt, 30 g (1 oz) ricotta, 2 teaspoons olive oil and the broad beans. → **1 X 100 G (3½ OZ) CONTAINER (TUESDAY DINNER)**

7. Chocolate pudding

⏲ 15 mins

Whisk 100 ml (3½ fl oz) milk with 1 tablespoon cornflour and 1 teaspoon sugar. Add 100 ml (3½ fl oz) milk, mix together and cook over low heat, stirring until thick and creamy. Remove from the heat and add the chocolate in pieces, whisking in well. Pour into a ramekin and let it cool. → **KEEP UP TO 48 HRS IN THE REFRIGERATOR (MONDAY SNACK)**

8. Store

⏲ 5 minutes

STORING Clearly label → Monday's portions in the refrigerator and other portions in the freezer.
LEFTOVERS Freeze any extras in ice cube trays or in other suitable containers. Store left-over chicken in 20–25 g (¾–1 oz) portions in bags or other containers. → **FREEZER**

Tuna niçoise / Chocolate pudding / Gazpacho

⏱ Ready in 10 mins

LUNCH Reheat the portion of tuna with vegetables. Offer fresh fruit for dessert.
SNACK Serve a chocolate pudding.
DINNER Serve the gazpacho cold with small pieces of cucumber on the side and some bread with about 30 g (1 oz) ricotta cheese. Serve some cooked fruit for dessert.

Roast chicken and vegetables with couscous / Raspberry 'ice cream' / Pasta and creamy pesto

🕐 Ready in 10 minutes (15 minutes for dinner)

LUNCH Cook 25 g (1 oz) couscous. Reheat the chicken and vegetables and serve with the couscous. Offer fresh fruit for dessert.
SNACK Process 70–100 g (2½–3½ oz) yoghurt with the frozen raspberries to make a sort of ice cream.
DINNER Cook 30–40 g (1–1½ oz) pasta and serve with the basil and ricotta pesto sauce.

Melon salad / Banana and blackberry smoothie / Beans in tomato sauce

🕐 Ready in 10 mins

LUNCH Cube or ball 1 slice of rockmelon. Mix with halved cherry tomatoes and the bocconcini balls. Dress with some olive oil, a tiny pinch of salt and a little torn basil.

SNACK Purée ½ banana with the blackberries, milk and about 50 g (1¾ oz) yoghurt.

DINNER Drain and rinse the tinned beans and heat them in a portion of tomato coulis. Serve with a slice of lightly toasted bread.

Rice, chicken and summer vegetables / Strawberries on bread / Gazpacho

🕐 Ready in 10 minutes (15 minutes for lunch)

LUNCH Cook 30 g (1 oz) rice and serve with the reheated chicken and vegetables.
SNACK Lightly butter a slice of sandwich bread and arrange slices of strawberry on top. Sprinkle with a little vanilla sugar and a few drops of lime (which will be used again the next day).
DINNER Serve the gazpacho with a little left-over rice from lunch sautéed in a little olive oil, if it hasn't been used up, or some bread and a piece of emmental or cheddar cheese.

Friday

Tuna niçoise / Fruit salad / Pasta and tomato sauce

🕐 Ready in 15 mins

LUNCH Reheat the tuna with vegetables.
SNACK Make balls or cubes of rockmelon and watermelon. Add some quartered strawberries and season with small mint leaves and a few drops of lime.
DINNER Cook 30–40 g (1–1½ oz) pasta and serve with the tomato coulis and some grated parmesan cheese if you like.

Peach charlotte

🕐 Ready in 20 min + 3–4 hours resting time

Heat 400 ml (14 fl oz) water and dissolve 150 g (5½ oz) of sugar in it. Cook 5 peaches in the syrup until they are tender (5–10 minutes). Reserve the syrup. Peel and halve the peaches, remove the stones and purée in a blender or food processor. Whisk 240 g (8½ oz) ricotta and mix with the peach purée and 100 ml (3½ fl oz) whipped cream. Dip the sponge finger biscuits in the syrup, and use them to line a small charlotte mould (or another container with fairly high sides). Fill with the peach mixture, top with more biscuits and leave to set in the refrigerator for a few hours before unmoulding. You can also use the baked peach purée and vary the fruit.

Create your own batches

Want to compose your own meal plans?

To help you, there's a checklist of the ingredients for each recipe on the following pages, so you can create all the combinations you like and freely put together your baby's weekly meal plan.

MEAL PLANS 6–9 MONTHS

Meat and fish

Orange chicken, fennel and carrot (WEEK 1)
makes about 5 serves

FRUIT, VEGETABLES AND HERBS
- ❑ 600 g (1 lb 5 oz) carrots
- ❑ 600 g (1 lb 5 oz) fennel
- ❑ 10 coriander (cilantro) leaves
- ❑ ½ teaspoon onion
- ❑ 1 teaspoon orange juice
- ❑ for the version with green beans, replace the carrots and fennel with 600 g (1 lb 5 oz) green beans

REFRIGERATED
- ❑ 50 g (1¾ oz) chicken

GROCERIES
- ❑ 2 teaspoons olive oil

Cod, sweet potato and broccoli (WEEK 1)
makes about 5 serves

FRUIT, VEGETABLES AND HERBS
- ❑ 600 g (1 lb 5 oz) broccoli
- ❑ 600 g (1 lb 5 oz) sweet potato
- ❑ a little garlic
- ❑ 1 sprig dill

REFRIGERATED
- ❑ 50 g (1¾ oz) cod

GROCERIES
- ❑ 1 teaspoon olive oil
- ❑ 1 pinch paprika
- ❑ 1 pinch cumin

Turkey and chestnuts with celeriac and potatoes (WEEK 2)
makes about 5 serves

FRUIT, VEGETABLES AND HERBS
- ❑ 600 g (1 lb 5 oz) celeriac
- ❑ 600 g (1 lb 5 oz) potatoes
- ❑ ½ teaspoon French shallot
- ❑ 50 g (1¾ oz) vacuum-packed or bottled chestnuts
- ❑ a little parsley

REFRIGERATED
- ❑ 50 g (1¾ oz) turkey steak
- ❑ 1 teaspoon butter
- ❑ a little milk

GROCERIES
- ❑ 2 teaspoons olive oil

Herbed salmon with cauliflower and spinach purée (WEEK 2)
makes about 5 serves

FRUIT, VEGETABLES AND HERBS
- ❑ 4–5 sprigs parsley
- ❑ 4–5 chives
- ❑ 750 g (1 lb 10 oz) cauliflower
- ❑ 250 g (9 oz) frozen spinach

REFRIGERATED
- ❑ 50 g (1¾ oz) salmon, preferably wild
- ❑ a little milk

GROCERIES
- ❑ a little nutmeg
- ❑ 1 pinch sugar
- ❑ 2 teaspoons olive oil

Ratatouille and sea bream (WEEK 3)
makes about 5 serves

FRUIT, VEGETABLES AND HERBS
- ❑ 550 g (1 lb 4 oz) zucchini (courgette)
- ❑ 250 g (9 oz) eggplant (aubergine)
- ❑ 300 g (10½ oz) tomatoes

REFRIGERATED
- ❑ 50 g (1¾ oz) sea bream

GROCERIES
- ❑ 2 teaspoons olive oil
- ❑ a few basil leaves

Veal and green vegetables (WEEK 3)
makes about 3 serves

FRUIT, VEGETABLES AND HERBS
- ❑ 150 g (5½ oz) broad beans
- ❑ 180 g (6 oz) green beans
- ❑ 180 g (6 oz) potatoes
- ❑ 180 g (6 oz) zucchini (courgette)
- ❑ 5–6 basil leaves
- ❑ 1 mint leaf

REFRIGERATED
- ❑ 30 g (1 oz) veal

GROCERIES
- ❑ 2 tablespoons olive oil

Veal and ratatouille (WEEK 3)
makes about 5 serves

FRUIT, VEGETABLES AND HERBS
- ❑ 550 g (1 lb 4 oz) zucchini (courgette)
- ❑ 250 g (9 oz) eggplant (aubergine)
- ❑ 300 g (10½ oz) tomatoes

REFRIGERATED
- ❑ 50 g (1¾ oz) veal

GROCERIES
- ❑ 2 teaspoons olive oil
- ❑ a few basil leaves

Beef, carrots and parsnip (WEEK 4)
makes about 3 serves

FRUIT, VEGETABLES AND HERBS
- ❑ 500 g (1 lb 2 oz) carrots
- ❑ 180 g (6 oz) parsnips
- ❑ 1 small onion

REFRIGERATED
- ❑ 30 g (1 oz) minced beef

GROCERIES
- ❑ 2 teaspoons olive oil
- ❑ 2 sprigs chervil

Tuna with curried sweet potato and zucchini (WEEK 4)
makes about 3 serves

FRUIT, VEGETABLES AND HERBS
- ❑ 330 g (11½ oz) sweet potato
- ❑ 330 g (11½ oz) zucchini (courgette)
- ❑ 1 sprig chervil
- ❑ 2–3 chives

REFRIGERATED
- ❑ 30 g (1 oz) tuna
- ❑ 10 g (¼ oz) butter

GROCERIES
- ❑ 1 pinch curry powder
- ❑ 1 teaspoon olive oil

Beef, pumpkin and silverbeet (WEEK 4)
makes about 3 serves

FRUIT, VEGETABLES AND HERBS
- ❑ 500 g (1 lb 2 oz) pumpkin
- ❑ 200 g (7 oz) silverbeet
- ❑ 1 sprig chervil
- ❑ 2–3 chives
- ❑ 1 small onion

REFRIGERATED
- ❑ 30 g (1 oz) minced beef
- ❑ 1 teaspoon butter

GROCERIES
- ❑ 1 teaspoon olive oil

Starchy foods

Semolina with cheese (WEEK 1)
makes 1 serve

REFRIGERATED
- ❑ 10–15 g (¼–½ oz) parmesan cheese

GROCERIES
- ❑ 25 g (1 oz) very fine semolina

MEAL PLANS 6–9 MONTHS *CONTINUED*

Semolina and tomato (WEEK 3)
makes I serve

FRUIT, VEGETABLES AND HERBS
- ❏ 120 g (4¼ oz) tomatoes

REFRIGERATED
- ❏ 10–15 g (¼–½ oz) parmesan or other cheese

GROCERIES
- ❏ 25 g (1 oz) very fine semolina

Polenta and cheese (WEEK 4)
makes I serve

REFRIGERATED
- ❏ 100 ml (3½ fl oz) milk
- ❏ 10 g (¼ oz) grated parmesan cheese

GROCERIES
- ❏ 30 g (1 oz) polenta

Vegetables

Broccoli soup (WEEK 1)
makes about 2 serves

FRUIT, VEGETABLES AND HERBS
- ❏ 420 g (14¾ oz) broccoli

GROCERIES
- ❏ 1 teaspoon olive oil

Broccoli and sweet potato soup (WEEK 1)
makes about 2 serves

FRUIT, VEGETABLES AND HERBS
- ❏ 220 g (7¾ oz) broccoli
- ❏ 220 g (7¾ oz) sweet potato

GROCERIES
- ❏ 1 teaspoon olive oil

Green bean purée (WEEK 1)
makes about 2 serves

FRUIT, VEGETABLES AND HERBS
- ❏ 450 g (1 lb) green beans

GROCERIES
- ❏ 1 teaspoon olive oil

Fennel and sweet potato purée (WEEK 1)
makes about 2 serves

FRUIT, VEGETABLES AND HERBS
- ❏ 220 g (7¾ oz) fennel
- ❏ 220 g (7¾ oz) sweet potato

GROCERIES
- ❏ 1 teaspoon olive oil

Creamy guacamole (WEEK 1)
for the whole family to share

FRUIT, VEGETABLES AND HERBS
- ❏ 1 avocado
- ❏ a dash of lime juice
- ❏ 5–6 coriander (cilantro) leaves

REFRIGERATED
- ❏ 60 g (2¼ oz) cream cheese or thick yoghurt

GROCERIES
- ❏ 1 pinch cumin
- ❏ 1 pinch sweet paprika

Cauliflower and spinach soup (WEEK 2)
makes about 2 serves

FRUIT, VEGETABLES AND HERBS
- ❏ 200 g (7 oz) cauliflower
- ❏ 50 g (1¾ oz) frozen spinach

GROCERIES
- ❏ 1 teaspoon olive oil

Carrot and corn soup (WEEK 2)
makes about 5 serves

FRUIT, VEGETABLES AND HERBS
- ❏ 150 g (5½ oz) corn kernels
- ❏ 400 g (14 oz) carrots

GROCERIES
- ❏ 1 teaspoon olive oil

Celeriac and apple soup (WEEK 2)
makes about 3 serves

FRUIT, VEGETABLES AND HERBS
- ❏ 300 g (10½ oz) celeriac
- ❏ 60 g (2¼ oz) apple purée

GROCERIES
- ❏ 1 teaspoon olive oil

Broad and green bean soup (WEEK 3)
makes about 2 serves

FRUIT, VEGETABLES AND HERBS
- ❏ 220 g (7¾ oz) broad beans
- ❏ 220 g (7¾ oz) green beans
- ❏ 2–3 mint leaves

GROCERIES
- ❏ 1 teaspoon olive oil

Gazpacho (WEEK 3)
makes I serve

FRUIT, VEGETABLES AND HERBS
- ❏ 50 g (1¾ oz) cucumber
- ❏ 50 g (1¾ oz) tomato
- ❏ 2–3 basil leaves
- ❏ a little garlic
- ❏ a little onion

Zucchini and basil purée (WEEK 3)
makes about 2 serves

FRUIT, VEGETABLES AND HERBS
- ❏ 450 g (1 lb) zucchini (courgette)
- ❏ 25 basil leaves

GROCERIES
- ❏ 1 teaspoon olive oil

Tomato soup (WEEK 3)
makes about 2 serves

FRUIT, VEGETABLES AND HERBS
- ❏ 450 g (1 lb) tomatoes
- ❏ 5–6 basil leaves

GROCERIES
- ❏ 2 teaspoons olive oil

Baba ghanoush (WEEK 3)
makes about 3 serves

FRUIT, VEGETABLES AND HERBS
- ❏ 100 g (3½ oz) cooked eggplant (aubergine)
- ❏ 30 g (1 oz) fresh tomato purée
- ❏ 1 pinch garlic

REFRIGERATED
- ❏ 30 g (1 oz) yoghurt

Zucchini and silverbeet soup (WEEK 4)
makes about 2 serves

FRUIT, VEGETABLES AND HERBS
- ❏ 220 g (7¾ oz) zucchini (courgette)
- ❏ 220 g (7¾ oz) silverbeet
- ❏ 1 sprig chervil
- ❏ 3 chives

GROCERIES
- ❏ 2 teaspoons olive oil

Parsnip and apple soup (WEEK 4)
makes about 3 serves

FRUIT, VEGETABLES AND HERBS
- ❏ 300 g (10½ oz) parsnips
- ❏ 60 g (2¼ oz) apple purée

GROCERIES
- ❏ 1 teaspoon olive oil

Zucchini and herb purée
(WEEK 4)
makes about 2 serves

FRUIT, VEGETABLES AND HERBS
- ❏ 450 g (1 lb) zucchini (courgette)
- ❏ 1 sprig chervil
- ❏ 3 chives

GROCERIES
- ❏ 1 teaspoon olive oil

Carrot and chervil purée
(WEEK 4)
makes about 2 serves

FRUIT, VEGETABLES AND HERBS
- ❏ 450 g (1 lb) carrots
- ❏ 2 sprigs chervil

GROCERIES
- ❏ 1 teaspoon olive oil

Desserts

Apple purée (WEEK 1)
makes about 5 serves

FRUIT, VEGETABLES AND HERBS
- ❏ 600 g (1 lb 5 oz) apples

GROCERIES
- ❏ ½ vanilla bean or 1 pinch cinnamon

Banana and cinnamon (WEEK 1)
makes 1 serve

FRUIT, VEGETABLES AND HERBS
- ❏ ½–1 banana

REFRIGERATED
- ❏ 20–50 g (¾–1¾ oz) yoghurt

GROCERIES
- ❏ 1 pinch cinnamon

Pear purée (WEEK 1)
makes about 5 serves

FRUIT, VEGETABLES AND HERBS
- ❏ 600 g (1 lb 5 oz) pears

GROCERIES
- ❏ ½ vanilla bean or 1 pinch cinnamon

Apple and pear purée
(WEEK 1)
makes about 5 serves

FRUIT, VEGETABLES AND HERBS
- ❏ 300 g (10½ oz) apples
- ❏ 300 g (10½ oz) pears

GROCERIES
- ❏ ½ vanilla bean or 1 pinch cinnamon

Mango smoothie
(WEEK 2)
makes 1 serve

FRUIT, VEGETABLES AND HERBS
- ❏ 100 g (3½ oz) peeled mango

REFRIGERATED
- ❏ 1 small tub yoghurt
- ❏ a little milk

Apple and mango purée
(WEEK 2)
makes 5 serves

FRUIT, VEGETABLES AND HERBS
- ❏ 300 g (10½ oz) apples
- ❏ 300 g (10½ oz) mango

Steamed banana
(WEEK 2)
makes 1 serve

FRUIT, VEGETABLES AND HERBS
- ❏ 1 banana
- ❏ juice of 1 orange

GROCERIES
- ❏ 1 star anise

Peach purée (WEEK 3)
makes about 5 serves

FRUIT, VEGETABLES AND HERBS
- ❏ 600 g (1 lb 5 oz) peaches

Peach and apricot purée
(WEEK 3)
makes about 5 serves

FRUIT, VEGETABLES AND HERBS
- ❏ 300 g (10½ oz) peaches
- ❏ 300 g (10½ oz) apricots

Strawberry smoothie
(WEEK 3)
makes 1 serve

FRUIT, VEGETABLES AND HERBS
- ❏ 100 g (3½ oz) strawberries

REFRIGERATED
- ❏ 50 g (1¾ oz) yoghurt
- ❏ a little milk

Strawberry and apricot purée (WEEK 3)
makes about 5 serves

FRUIT, VEGETABLES AND HERBS
- ❏ 300 g (10½ oz) strawberries
- ❏ 300 g (10½ oz) apricots

Apple and quince purée
(WEEK 4)
makes about 5 serves

FRUIT, VEGETABLES AND HERBS
- ❏ 300 g (10½ oz) apples
- ❏ 300 g (10½ oz) quince

GROCERIES
- ❏ ½ vanilla bean

Apple and clementine purée
(WEEK 4)
makes about 5 serves

FRUIT, VEGETABLES AND HERBS
- ❏ 300 g (10½ oz) apples
- ❏ 300 g (10½ oz) clementines

GROCERIES
- ❏ ½ vanilla bean

Kiwifruit and banana smoothie (WEEK 4)
makes 1 serve

FRUIT, VEGETABLES AND HERBS
- ❏ 1 kiwifruit
- ❏ ½ banana
- ❏ 2–3 mint leaves
- ❏ a few drops of lemon juice

MEAL PLANS 9–12 MONTHS

Meat and fish

Fish and ratatouille
(WEEK 1)
makes about 3 serves

FRUIT, VEGETABLES AND HERBS
- ❏ 100 g (3½ oz) eggplant (aubergine)
- ❏ 300 g (10½ oz) zucchini (courgette)
- ❏ 300 g (10½ oz) tomatoes
- ❏ a little garlic
- ❏ 4–5 basil leaves
- ❏ a few thyme leaves

REFRIGERATED
- ❏ 45 g (1½ oz) white fish fillet

GROCERIES
- ❏ 2 teaspoons olive oil

Chicken and green vegetables (WEEK 1)
makes 3 or 4 serves

FRUIT, VEGETABLES AND HERBS
- ❏ 250 g (9 oz) zucchini (courgette)
- ❏ 300 g (10½ oz) green beans
- ❏ 125 g (4½ oz) fennel
- ❏ 100 g (3½ oz) spinach
- ❏ ½ French shallot
- ❏ 5–6 basil leaves

REFRIGERATED
- ❏ 60 g (2¼ oz) chicken

GROCERIES
- ❏ 2 teaspoons olive oil

Fish, mashed potato and zucchini (WEEK 1)
makes about 3 serves

FRUIT, VEGETABLES AND HERBS
- ❏ 350 g (12 oz) potatoes
- ❏ 350 g (12 oz) zucchini (courgette)
- ❏ 100 g (3½ oz) frozen spinach
- ❏ ½ French shallot
- ❏ 3–4 basil leaves

REFRIGERATED
- ❏ 45 g (1½ oz) white fish fillet
- ❏ 1 teaspoon butter

GROCERIES
- ❏ 2 teaspoons olive oil

Beef and tomato stew with potatoes
(WEEK 2)
makes about 3 serves

FRUIT, VEGETABLES AND HERBS
- ❏ 500 g (1 lb 2 oz) potatoes
- ❏ 250 g (9 oz) tomatoes
- ❏ 5–6 basil leaves
- ❏ 1 small onion

REFRIGERATED
- ❏ 50 g (1¾ oz) beef
- ❏ 10 g (¼ oz) butter

GROCERIES
- ❏ 1 teaspoon olive oil

Cod with herb and lemon crust and broccoli purée
(WEEK 2)
makes about 3 serves

FRUIT, VEGETABLES AND HERBS
- ❏ 600 g (1 lb 5 oz) broccoli
- ❏ 5 basil leaves
- ❏ ½ teaspoon fresh thyme
- ❏ 1 pinch lemon zest
- ❏ 2 teaspoons lemon juice

REFRIGERATED
- ❏ 50 g (1¾ oz) cod
- ❏ 10 g (¼ oz) butter

GROCERIES
- ❏ 1 packet melba toast or rusks
- ❏ 1 teaspoon olive oil

Salmon with spinach
(WEEK 2)
makes about 3 serves

FRUIT, VEGETABLES AND HERBS
- ❏ 150 g (5½ oz) frozen spinach
- ❏ 5 basil leaves
- ❏ ½ teaspoon fresh thyme
- ❏ 1 pinch lemon zest
- ❏ 2 teaspoons lemon juice

REFRIGERATED
- ❏ 50 g (1¾ oz) salmon
- ❏ 10 g (¼ oz) butter

GROCERIES
- ❏ 1 packet melba toast or rusks
- ❏ 1 teaspoon olive oil

Beef and mashed potato
(WEEK 2)
makes about 3 serves

FRUIT, VEGETABLES AND HERBS
- ❏ 500 g (1 lb 2 oz) potatoes
- ❏ 250 g (9 oz) tomatoes
- ❏ 1 small onion
- ❏ 5–6 basil leaves

REFRIGERATED
- ❏ 50 g (1¾ oz) beef
- ❏ 10 g (¼ oz) butter

GROCERIES
- ❏ 1 teaspoon olive oil

Duck à l'orange
(WEEK 3)
makes about 3 serves

FRUIT, VEGETABLES AND HERBS
- ❏ 1 tablespoon orange juice

REFRIGERATED
- ❏ 50 g (1¾ oz) duck breast

GROCERIES
- ❏ a dash of honey
- ❏ 1 teaspoon olive oil

Orange fish
(WEEK 3)
makes about 3 serves

FRUIT, VEGETABLES AND HERBS
- ❏ 2 teaspoons orange juice
- ❏ a dash lemon juice
- ❏ 5 sprigs coriander (cilantro)

REFRIGERATED
- ❏ 50 g (1¾ oz) white fish fillet

GROCERIES
- ❏ 2 teaspoons olive oil

Veal navarin
(WEEK 4)
makes about 4 serves

FRUIT, VEGETABLES AND HERBS
- ❏ 120 g (4¼ oz) carrots
- ❏ 220 g (7¾ oz) zucchini (courgette)
- ❏ 50 g (1¾ oz) turnip
- ❏ 100 g (3½ oz) peas
- ❏ 2 bulb spring onions (scallions)

REFRIGERATED
- ❏ 60 g (2¼ oz) veal
- ❏ 10 g (¼ oz) butter

GROCERIES
- ❏ 2 teaspoons oil
- ❏ 10 g (¼ oz) plain flour
- ❏ ½ organic vegetable stock cube

Sole fish cakes
(WEEK 4)
makes about 3 serves

FRUIT, VEGETABLES AND HERBS
- ❏ 50 g (1¾ oz) mashed potato

REFRIGERATED
- ❏ 50 g (1¾ oz) cooked sole fillet
- ❏ a little chervil

GROCERIES
- ❏ 2 teaspoons oil

Sole with chervil and zucchini
(WEEK 4)
makes about 3 serves

FRUIT, VEGETABLES AND HERBS
- ❏ 200 g (7 oz) zucchini (courgette)
- ❏ 3 sprigs chervil
- ❏ 3 sprigs coriander (cilantro)

REFRIGERATED
- ❏ 50 g (1¾ oz) sole

GROCERIES
- ❏ 2 teaspoons oil

Vegetables and starchy foods

Zucchini risotto
(WEEK 1)
makes 1 serve

FRUIT, VEGETABLES AND HERBS
- ❏ 100 g (3½ oz) zucchini (courgette) and spinach purée
- ❏ 1 small French shallot

REFRIGERATED
- ❏ 1 teaspoon butter
- ❏ ½ teaspoon crème fraîche
- ❏ 10 g (¼ oz) parmesan cheese

GROCERIES
- ❏ 20 g (¾ oz) short-grain rice
- ❏ ½ organic vegetable stock cube

Lentil, zucchini and spinach soup
(WEEK 1)
makes about 2 serves

FRUIT, VEGETABLES AND HERBS
- ❏ 40 g (1½ oz) lentils
- ❏ 120 g (4¼ oz) zucchini (courgette)
- ❏ 120 g (4¼ oz) frozen spinach
- ❏ 4–5 basil leaves

GROCERIES
- ❏ 1 teaspoon oil
- ❏ ½ organic stock cube, crumbled

Lentils and ratatouille with fromage frais (WEEK 1)
makes about 3 serves

FRUIT, VEGETABLES AND HERBS
- ❏ 100 g eggplant (aubergine)
- ❏ 300 g (10½ oz) zucchini (courgette)
- ❏ 300 g (10½ oz) tomatoes
- ❏ 4–5 basil leaves
- ❏ a few thyme leaves
- ❏ a little garlic

REFRIGERATED
- ❏ 60 g (2¼ oz) fromage frais or cream cheese

GROCERIES
- ❏ 50 g (1¾ oz) lentils
- ❏ 1 teaspoon olive oil

Zucchini, spinach and potato soup (WEEK 1)
makes about 2 serves

FRUIT, VEGETABLES AND HERBS
- ❏ 150 g (5½ oz) zucchini (courgette)
- ❏ 50 g (1¾ oz) spinach
- ❏ 150 g (5½ oz) potatoes
- ❏ 3–4 basil leaves

GROCERIES
- ❏ 2 teaspoons olive oil

Rice and broccoli purée
(WEEK 2)
makes 1 serve

FRUIT, VEGETABLES AND HERBS
- ❏ 100 g (3½ oz) broccoli purée
- ❏ 1 small French shallot

REFRIGERATED
- ❏ 1 teaspoon butter
- ❏ ½ teaspoon crème fraîche
- ❏ 10 g (¼ oz) parmesan cheese

GROCERIES
- ❏ 20 g (¾ oz) short-grain rice
- ❏ ½ organic vegetable stock cube

Pasta and tomato sauce
(WEEK 2)
makes 1 serve

FRUIT, VEGETABLES AND HERBS
- ❏ 120 g (4¼ oz) tomatoes
- ❏ 4–5 basil leaves
- ❏ ¼ small onion

REFRIGERATED
- ❏ 15–20 g (½–¾ oz) parmesan cheese

GROCERIES
- ❏ 15–20 g (½–¾ oz) pasta
- ❏ 2 teaspoons olive oil

Pumpkin, carrot and coconut stew (WEEK 2)
makes about 3 serves

FRUIT, VEGETABLES AND HERBS
- ❏ 300 g (10½ oz) pumpkin
- ❏ 300 g (10½ oz) carrots
- ❏ one-third of a leek
- ❏ 1 pinch ginger
- ❏ 1 pinch garlic
- ❏ 1 small onion

GROCERIES
- ❏ 30 ml (1 fl oz) coconut milk
- ❏ ½ stock cube, crumbled
- ❏ 1 teaspoon olive oil
- ❏ 1 pinch curry powder

Corn and tomato soup
(WEEK 2)
makes about 2 serves

FRUIT, VEGETABLES AND HERBS
- ❏ 120 g (4¼ oz) tomatoes
- ❏ 120 g (4¼ oz) corn kernels
- ❏ ¼ small onion

GROCERIES
- ❏ 1 pinch cumin
- ❏ 1 pinch paprika
- ❏ 2 teaspoons olive oil

Pasta and broccoli
(WEEK 2)
makes 1 serve

FRUIT, VEGETABLES AND HERBS
- ❏ 120 g (4¼ oz) broccoli
- ❏ 4–5 basil leaves

REFRIGERATED
- ❏ 15–20 g (½–¾ oz) parmesan cheese

GROCERIES
- ❏ 15–20 g (½–¾ oz) pasta
- ❏ 2 teaspoons olive oil

Carrot, celeriac and turnip purée (WEEK 3)
makes about 3 serves

FRUIT, VEGETABLES AND HERBS
- ❏ ¼ small onion
- ❏ 200 g (7 oz) carrots
- ❏ 100 g (3½ oz) turnips
- ❏ 100 g (3½ oz) celeriac

REFRIGERATED
- ❏ 10 g (¼ oz) butter

GROCERIES
- ❏ 2 teaspoons olive oil

MEAL PLANS 9–12 MONTHS *CONTINUED*

Potato and leek soup
(WEEK 3)
makes about 3 large serves

FRUIT, VEGETABLES AND HERBS
- ❑ 300 g (10½ oz) leek
- ❑ 300 g (10½ oz) potatoes
- ❑ ½ onion

REFRIGERATED
- ❑ 15 g (½ oz) emmental or cheddar cheese

GROCERIES
- ❑ 1 teaspoon oil
- ❑ ½ organic stock cube, crumbled

Mashed potato with watercress **(WEEK 3)**
makes about 3 large serves

FRUIT, VEGETABLES AND HERBS
- ❑ ½ bunch watercress
- ❑ 500 g (1 lb 2 oz) potatoes
- ❑ ½ onion

REFRIGERATED
- ❑ 10 g (½ oz) butter

GROCERIES
- ❑ 1 teaspoon olive oil

Vegetable stew with almonds
(WEEK 3)
makes about 4 large serves

FRUIT, VEGETABLES AND HERBS
- ❑ 220 g (7¾ oz) carrots
- ❑ 220 g (7¾ oz) celeriac
- ❑ 220 g (7¾ oz) turnips
- ❑ 220 g (7¾ oz) potatoes
- ❑ 1 small onion
- ❑ 1 pinch grated garlic

GROCERIES
- ❑ 50 g (1¾ oz) ground almonds
- ❑ ½ teaspoon curry powder
- ❑ 2 teaspoons oil

Pasta with watercress and cheese **(WEEK 3)**
makes 1 serve

FRUIT, VEGETABLES AND HERBS
- ❑ 50 g (1¾ oz) mashed potato and watercress

REFRIGERATED
- ❑ 15–20 g (½–¾ oz) emmental or cheddar cheese
- ❑ 10 g (¼ oz) butter

GROCERIES
- ❑ 15–20 g (½–¾ oz) pasta

Polenta and cheese **(WEEK 3)**
makes 1 serve

REFRIGERATED
- ❑ 120 ml (3¾ fl oz) milk
- ❑ 10 g (¼ oz) emmental or cheddar cheese

GROCERIES
- ❑ 20 g (¾ oz) polenta

Asparagus and pea risotto
(WEEK 4)
makes 1 serve

FRUIT, VEGETABLES AND HERBS
- ❑ 100 g (3½ oz) asparagus and pea purée
- ❑ 1 small French shallot

REFRIGERATED
- ❑ 1 teaspoon butter
- ❑ ½ teaspoon crème fraîche
- ❑ 10 g (¼ oz) parmesan cheese

GROCERIES
- ❑ 20 g (¾ oz) short-grain rice
- ❑ ½ organic vegetable stock cube

Zucchini and parmesan flan
(WEEK 4)
makes 2 flans

FRUIT, VEGETABLES AND HERBS
- ❑ 300 g (10½ oz) zucchini (courgette)
- ❑ 4 sprigs coriander (cilantro)
- ❑ 2 sprigs chervil

REFRIGERATED
- ❑ 1 egg
- ❑ 30 g (1 oz) grated parmesan cheese
- ❑ 50 ml (1½ fl oz) milk
- ❑ butter, for the tin

GROCERIES
- ❑ 1 teaspoon olive oil

Carrot and coriander soup with fromage frais
(WEEK 4)
makes about 3 serves

FRUIT, VEGETABLES AND HERBS
- ❑ 300 g (10½ oz) carrots
- ❑ 100 g (3½ oz) turnips
- ❑ 10 coriander (cilantro) leaves

REFRIGERATED
- ❑ 30 g (1 oz) fromage frais or cream cheese

GROCERIES
- ❑ 2 teaspoons olive oil

Pasta with peas **(WEEK 4)**
makes 1 serve

FRUIT, VEGETABLES AND HERBS
- ❑ 50 g (1¾ oz) asparagus
- ❑ 50 g (1¾ oz) peas
- ❑ 3–4 mint leaves

REFRIGERATED
- ❑ 15–20 g (½–¾ oz) parmesan cheese

GROCERIES
- ❑ 15–20 g (½–¾ oz) pasta
- ❑ 2 teaspoons olive oil

Green lentil and zucchini soup **(WEEK 4)**
makes about 2 serves

FRUIT, VEGETABLES AND HERBS
- ❑ 40 g (1½ oz) tomato purée
- ❑ 100 g (3½ oz) zucchini (courgette)
- ❑ 10 coriander (cilantro) leaves

REFRIGERATED
- ❑ 30 g (1 oz) fromage frais or cream cheese

GROCERIES
- ❑ 2 teaspoons olive oil
- ❑ 40 g (1½ oz) green lentils

Desserts

Melon and orange flower yoghurt **(WEEK 1)**
makes 1 serve

FRUIT, VEGETABLES AND HERBS
- ❑ 1 slice melon

REFRIGERATED
- ❑ 1 small tub yoghurt

GROCERIES
- ❑ a few drops of orange flower water

Porridge **(WEEK 1)**

REFRIGERATED
- ❑ 90 ml (3 fl oz) milk

GROCERIES
- ❑ 20 g (¾ oz) baby oat flakes
- ❑ 1 pinch cinnamon

Apple and plum purée
(WEEK 2)
makes about 5 serves

FRUIT, VEGETABLES AND HERBS
- ❑ 300 g (10½ oz) apples
- ❑ 300 g (10½ oz) plums

GROCERIES
- ❑ 1 pinch cinnamon

Plum smoothie
(WEEK 2)
makes 1 serve

FRUIT, VEGETABLES AND HERBS
- ❏ 100 g (3½ oz) plum purée

REFRIGERATED
- ❏ 70–100 g (2½–3½ oz) yoghurt

Plum purée
(WEEK 2)
makes about 5 serves

FRUIT, VEGETABLES AND HERBS
- ❏ 600 g (1 lb 5 oz) plums

GROCERIES
- ❏ 1 pinch cinnamon

Pineapple purée
(WEEK 2)
makes about 5 serves

FRUIT, VEGETABLES AND HERBS
- ❏ 600 g (1 lb 5 oz) pineapple

GROCERIES
- ❏ ½ vanilla bean or 1 pinch ginger

Pancakes
(WEEK 2)

REFRIGERATED
- ❏ 1 egg
- ❏ a little butter

GROCERIES
- ❏ 50 ml (1½ fl oz) coconut milk
- ❏ 60 g (2¼ oz) plain flour

Semolina pudding
(WEEKS 2 AND 3)
makes 1 serve

REFRIGERATED
- ❏ 200 ml (7 fl oz) milk

GROCERIES
- ❏ a few drops of orange flower water
- ❏ 20 g (¾ oz) fine semolina

Fruit salad
(WEEK 3)

FRUIT, VEGETABLES AND HERBS
- ❏ 1 clementine
- ❏ ¼ banana
- ❏ juice of ½ orange
- ❏ ¼ pear

Sponge fingers
(WEEK 3)

FRUIT, VEGETABLES AND HERBS
- ❏ 2 teaspoons lemon juice
- ❏ 1 pinch lemon zest

REFRIGERATED
- ❏ 30 g (1 oz) butter
- ❏ 1 egg

GROCERIES
- ❏ 1 pinch baking powder
- ❏ 125 g (4½ oz) plain flour
- ❏ 2 tablespoons sugar
- ❏ 2 teaspoons olive oil

Fruit mousse
(WEEKS 3 AND 4)
makes 1 serve

FRUIT, VEGETABLES AND HERBS
- ❏ 100 g (3½ oz) fruit purée (apple, apple and rhubarb)

REFRIGERATED
- ❏ 1 small tub yoghurt

Rice pudding
(WEEK 4)
makes 1 serve

REFRIGERATED
- ❏ 200 ml (7 fl oz) milk

GROCERIES
- ❏ ½ vanilla bean
- ❏ 20 g (¾ oz) rice

Muffins
(WEEK 4)

REFRIGERATED
- ❏ 10 g (¼ oz) butter

GROCERIES
- ❏ 40 g (1½ oz) plain flour
- ❏ 1 pinch baking powder
- ❏ 1 teaspoon sugar
- ❏ 60 g (2¼ oz) your choice of fruit purée

MEAL PLANS 12 MONTHS+

Meat and fish

Fish pie (WEEK 1)
makes 2 serves

FRUIT, VEGETABLES AND HERBS
- ❏ 120 g (4¼ oz) broccoli
- ❏ 150 g (5½ oz) cooked sweet potato
- ❏ 150 g (5½ oz) cooked potatoes
- ❏ 5 basil leaves
- ❏ a few drops of lemon juice

REFRIGERATED
- ❏ 50 g (1¾ oz) sea bream
- ❏ 10 g (¼ oz) butter
- ❏ 1 tablespoon cream
- ❏ a little milk

GROCERIES
- ❏ 1 pinch nutmeg
- ❏ 1 pinch salt

Meatballs in tomato sauce
(WEEK 1)
makes about 3 serves

FRUIT, VEGETABLES AND HERBS
- ❏ 50 g (1¾ oz) cooked potatoes
- ❏ 1 small onion
- ❏ 1 pinch grated garlic
- ❏ 10 basil leaves
- ❏ a little thyme

REFRIGERATED
- ❏ 50 g (1¾ oz) minced beef

GROCERIES
- ❏ 300 g (10½ oz) tinned tomatoes
- ❏ 3–4 teaspoons olive oil
- ❏ + 30 g (1 oz) rice or couscous to serve

Orange fish parcel
(WEEK 2)
makes 1 serve

FRUIT, VEGETABLES AND HERBS
- ❏ 1 slice orange
- ❏ 5–6 tender parsley leaves

REFRIGERATED
- ❏ 20–30 g (¾–1 oz) cod fillet

GROCERIES
- ❏ 1 teaspoon olive oil
- ❏ 1 tiny pinch salt

MEAL PLANS 12 MONTHS+ *CONTINUED*

Lamb tagine
(WEEK 2)
makes 2–3 serves

FRUIT, VEGETABLES AND HERBS
- ❏ 200 g (7 oz) carrots
- ❏ 5 dried apricots
- ❏ 1 garlic clove
- ❏ 1 pinch grated ginger

REFRIGERATED
- ❏ 50 g (1¾ oz) lamb leg

GROCERIES
- ❏ 100 g (3½ oz) tinned tomatoes
- ❏ ½ organic vegetable stock cube
- ❏ 1 pinch cumin
- ❏ 1 pinch cinnamon
- ❏ 1 tablespoon olive oil

Salmon and spinach lasagne
(WEEK 3)
makes 2 serves

FRUIT, VEGETABLES AND HERBS
- ❏ 100 g (3½ oz) frozen spinach
- ❏ 2 sprigs flat-leaf parsley
- ❏ 2 sprigs chervil

REFRIGERATED
- ❏ 50 g (1¾ oz) wild salmon
- ❏ 75 g (2½ oz) ricotta cheese
- ❏ 1 tablespoon pouring cream

GROCERIES
- ❏ ½ organic vegetable stock cube

Veal involtini with herbs
(WEEK 3)
makes 2–3 serves

FRUIT, VEGETABLES AND HERBS
- ❏ 2 sprigs flat-leaf parsley
- ❏ 2 sprigs chervil
- ❏ 2–3 sage leaves

REFRIGERATED
- ❏ 1 slice prosciutto
- ❏ 50 g (1¾ oz) veal steak
- ❏ 75 g (2½ oz) ricotta cheese

Tuna niçoise
(WEEK 4)
makes 2–3 serves

FRUIT, VEGETABLES AND HERBS
- ❏ 450 g (1 lb) baked tomatoes, zucchini (courgette), capsicum (pepper) and eggplant (aubergine)
- ❏ a little thyme

REFRIGERATED
- ❏ 50 g (1¾ oz) tuna

GROCERIES
- ❏ 2 teaspoons olive oil

Roast chicken and vegetables
(WEEK 4)
makes 5–6 serves

FRUIT, VEGETABLES AND HERBS
- ❏ 5 tomatoes
- ❏ 2–3 zucchini (courgette)
- ❏ 5 basil leaves
- ❏ a little grated garlic
- ❏ 1 small onion

REFRIGERATED
- ❏ 1 chicken thigh

GROCERIES
- ❏ 1 tablespoon oil
- ❏ 1 tiny pinch salt
- ❏ + 30 g (1 oz) rice or couscous to serve

Vegetables and starchy foods

Pasta with pumpkin and broccoli (WEEK 1)
makes 1 serve

FRUIT, VEGETABLES AND HERBS
- ❏ 120 g (4¼ oz) pumpkin
- ❏ 60 g (2¼ oz) broccoli

REFRIGERATED
- ❏ 15 g (½ oz) parmesan cheese
- ❏ a little cream

GROCERIES
- ❏ 20 g (¾ oz) pasta
- ❏ 2 tablespoons olive oil

Pumpkin and sweet potato soup
(WEEK 1)
makes about 3 serves

FRUIT, VEGETABLES AND HERBS
- ❏ 320 g (11¼ oz) butternut pumpkin
- ❏ 250 g (9 oz) sweet potato
- ❏ 1 small leek
- ❏ 1 small onion

REFRIGERATED
- ❏ 15–20 g (½–¾ oz) emmental or cheddar cheese

GROCERIES
- ❏ ½ organic stock cube
- ❏ 3 teaspoons olive oil
- ❏ for the garlic bread: bread, 1 small clove garlic

Egg-in-a-nest
(WEEK 1)
makes 3 serves

FRUIT, VEGETABLES AND HERBS
- ❏ 500 g (1 lb 2 oz) potatoes
- ❏ 200 g (7 oz) broccoli

REFRIGERATED
- ❏ 3 eggs
- ❏ 10 g (¼ oz) butter
- ❏ a little milk

Rice with broccoli
(WEEK 1)
makes 1 serve

FRUIT, VEGETABLES AND HERBS
- ❏ 150 g (5½ oz) broccoli
- ❏ a few drops of lemon juice

REFRIGERATED
- ❏ 1 tablespoon yoghurt

GROCERIES
- ❏ 1 teaspoon olive oil
- ❏ 20–30 g (¾–1 oz) rice
- ❏ ½ teaspoon tahini or almond butter

Pasta and tomato sauce
(WEEK 2)
makes 1 serve

FRUIT, VEGETABLES AND HERBS
- ❏ 150 g (5½ oz) tomatoes
- ❏ 4–5 basil leaves
- ❏ ¼ small onion

REFRIGERATED
- ❏ 15–20 g (½–¾ oz) parmesan cheese

GROCERIES
- ❏ 30–40 g (1–1½ oz) pasta
- ❏ 1 teaspoon olive oil

Leek and potato soup
(WEEK 2)
makes about 2 serves

FRUIT, VEGETABLES AND HERBS
- ❏ 300 g (10½ oz) leek
- ❏ 300 g (10½ oz) potatoes
- ❏ ½ onion
- ❏ a few chives

REFRIGERATED
- ❏ 1 spoonful crème fraîche

GROCERIES
- ❏ 1 teaspoon oil
- ❏ ½ organic stock cube, crumbled

Fried rice with egg
(WEEK 2)
makes 1 serve

FRUIT, VEGETABLES AND HERBS
- ❏ 60 g (2¼ oz) carrots
- ❏ 60 g (2¼ oz) cauliflower
- ❏ small piece fresh ginger

REFRIGERATED
- ❏ 1 egg

GROCERIES
- ❏ 2 teaspoons oil
- ❏ 30 ml (1 fl oz) coconut milk
- ❏ 60 g (2¼ oz) cooked rice – about 30 g (1 oz) raw rice

Red lentil soup (WEEK 2)
makes 2–3 serves

FRUIT, VEGETABLES AND HERBS
- ❏ a few drops lime juice
- ❏ 1 garlic clove
- ❏ 1 onion
- ❏ small piece fresh ginger

GROCERIES
- ❏ 20 g (¾ oz) red lentils
- ❏ 100 g (3½ oz) tinned tomatoes
- ❏ 60 ml (2 fl oz) coconut milk
- ❏ 1 pinch cumin
- ❏ 1 pinch cinnamon

Mashed potato and ham
(WEEK 2)
makes 1 serve

FRUIT, VEGETABLES AND HERBS
- ❏ 220 g (7¾ oz) potatoes

REFRIGERATED
- ❏ 20–30 g (¾–1 oz) ham
- ❏ 15 g (½ oz) butter
- ❏ 50 ml (1½ fl oz) milk

GROCERIES
- ❏ 1 tiny pinch salt

Spinach and zucchini
soup (WEEK 3)
makes about 3 serves

FRUIT, VEGETABLES AND HERBS
- ❏ 350 g (12 oz) zucchini (courgette)
- ❏ 200 g (7 oz) spinach
- ❏ 10 parsley leaves
- ❏ 2 sprigs chervil
- ❏ 1 small onion

GROCERIES
- ❏ 2 teaspoons olive oil
- ❏ ½ organic vegetable stock cube

Vegetable fritters
(WEEK 3)
makes about 2 serves

FRUIT, VEGETABLES AND HERBS
- ❏ 1 zucchini (courgette)
- ❏ 1 carrot

REFRIGERATED
- ❏ 1 egg
- ❏ 100–150 ml (3½–5 fl oz) milk
- ❏ a little butter

GROCERIES
- ❏ 100 g (3½ oz) plain flour

Pasta and green sauce
(WEEK 3)
makes 3 or 4 serves of sauce

FRUIT, VEGETABLES AND HERBS
- ❏ 400 g (14 oz) total of peas, snow peas, peeled broad beans
- ❏ 2 asparagus spears
- ❏ 1 small onion
- ❏ 1 garlic clove

GROCERIES
- ❏ 1 tablespoon olive oil
- ❏ ½ vegetable stock cube, crumbled
- ❏ + 15–20 g (½–¾ oz) pasta per serve

Gazpacho (WEEK 4)
makes 2–3 serves

FRUIT, VEGETABLES AND HERBS
- ❏ 320 g (11¼ oz) tomatoes
- ❏ ½ capsicum (pepper)
- ❏ ½ cucumber
- ❏ 1 small onion
- ❏ 5–6 basil leaves
- ❏ 1 pinch grated garlic

Creamy pesto (WEEK 4)
makes 1–2 serves

FRUIT, VEGETABLES AND HERBS
- ❏ 100 g (3½ oz) broad beans
- ❏ 1 bunch basil
- ❏ 1 pinch garlic

REFRIGERATED
- ❏ 30 g (1 oz) ricotta cheese
- ❏ 15 g (½ oz) parmesan cheese

GROCERIES
- ❏ 1 tablespoon olive oil
- ❏ 1 tiny pinch salt
- ❏ + 20 g (¾ oz) pasta per serve

Melon salad
(WEEK 4)
makes 1 serve

FRUIT, VEGETABLES AND HERBS
- ❏ 1 slice melon
- ❏ 100 g (3½ oz) cherry tomatoes
- ❏ 5–6 basil leaves

REFRIGERATED
- ❏ 5–6 bocconcini

GROCERIES
- ❏ 2 teaspoons olive oil

Beans in tomato sauce
(WEEK 4)
makes 1 serve

FRUIT, VEGETABLES AND HERBS
- ❏ 120 g (4¼ oz) tomatoes
- ❏ 3–4 basil leaves

REFRIGERATED
- ❏ 1 teaspoon butter

GROCERIES
- ❏ 1 teaspoon oil
- ❏ 100 g (3½ oz) tinned white beans, rinsed and drained
- ❏ 2 slices bread

Desserts

Baked custard
(WEEK 1)
makes 2–3 serves

REFRIGERATED
- ❏ 1 egg
- ❏ 200 ml (7 fl oz) milk

GROCERIES
- ❏ optional vanilla, orange flower water or clementine zest
- ❏ 1 tablespoon sugar

Swiss roll
(WEEK 1)

FRUIT, VEGETABLES AND HERBS
- ❏ 300 g (10½ oz) frozen raspberries

REFRIGERATED
- ❏ 2 eggs
- ❏ 500 ml (17 fl oz) milk
- ❏ a little thick yoghurt

GROCERIES
- ❏ 120 g (4¼ oz) sugar
- ❏ 150 g (5½ oz) plain flour
- ❏ 1 teaspoon baking powder

MEAL PLANS 12 MONTHS+ *CONTINUED*

Hot chocolate (WEEK 2)
makes 1 serve

REFRIGERATED
- ❏ 200 ml (7 fl oz) milk

GROCERIES
- ❏ 10–15 g (¼–½ oz) chocolate
- ❏ optional vanilla or cinnamon

Yoghurt cake
(WEEK 2)

FRUIT, VEGETABLES AND HERBS
- ❏ 1 pinch orange zest

REFRIGERATED
- ❏ 1 small tub yoghurt
- ❏ 2 eggs

GROCERIES
- ❏ 3 yoghurt tubs plain flour
- ❏ 1½ yoghurt tub sugar
- ❏ ½ yoghurt tub of neutral flavoured oil
- ❏ 1 teaspoon baking powder
- ❏ one tiny pinch salt

Fruit on bread
(WEEKS 2 AND 4)
makes 1 serve

FRUIT, VEGETABLES AND HERBS
- ❏ strawberries or banana

REFRIGERATED
- ❏ a little butter

GROCERIES
- ❏ 1 small slice sandwich bread
- ❏ 1 pinch cinnamon

Rhubarb purée
(WEEK 3)
makes about 5 serves

FRUIT, VEGETABLES AND HERBS
- ❏ 500 g (1 lb 2 oz) rhubarb

GROCERIES
- ❏ 60 g (2¼ oz) sugar

Mini bircher muesli
(WEEK 3)
makes 1 serve

FRUIT, VEGETABLES AND HERBS
- ❏ fresh fruit

REFRIGERATED
- ❏ milk

GROCERIES
- ❏ 15 g (½ oz) baby oat flakes
- ❏ 1 date or other dried fruit
- ❏ 1 pinch cinnamon

Chocolate yoghurt
(WEEK 3)
makes 1 serve

REFRIGERATED
- ❏ 1 small tub yoghurt

GROCERIES
- ❏ ½ teaspoon cocoa powder
- ❏ ½ teaspoon sugar

Mini trifle (WEEK 3)
makes about 2 serves

FRUIT, VEGETABLES AND HERBS
- ❏ 250 g (9 oz) strawberries
- ❏ Juice of 1 orange

REFRIGERATED
- ❏ 1 egg yolk
- ❏ 250 ml (9 fl oz) milk
- ❏ 100 ml (3½ fl oz) pouring cream
- ❏ 125 g (4½ oz) thick yoghurt

GROCERIES
- ❏ 10 g (¼ oz) cornflour
- ❏ 20 g (¾ oz) sugar
- ❏ 5 sponge finger biscuits

Raspberry 'ice cream'
(WEEK 4)
makes 1 serve

FRUIT, VEGETABLES AND HERBS
- ❏ 60 g (2¼ oz) frozen raspberries

REFRIGERATED
- ❏ 70–100 g (2½–3½ oz) yoghurt

Chocolate pudding
(WEEK 4)
makes 1–2 serves

REFRIGERATED
- ❏ 100 ml (3½ fl oz) milk

GROCERIES
- ❏ 20 g (¾ oz) chocolate
- ❏ 1 tablespoon cornflour
- ❏ 1 teaspoon sugar

Peach charlotte
(WEEK 4)

FRUIT, VEGETABLES AND HERBS
- ❏ 5 peaches

REFRIGERATED
- ❏ 240 g (8½ oz) ricotta cheese
- ❏ 100 ml (3½ fl oz) pouring cream

GROCERIES
- ❏ 15 small sponge finger biscuits
- ❏ 150 g (5½ oz) sugar

INDEX

Visit our website at www.skyhorsepublishing.com.

10 9 8 7 6 5 4 3 2 1

Library of Congress Cataloging-in-Publication Data is available on file.

Paperback ISBN: 978-1-5107-6852-9
Hardcover ISBN: 978-1-5107-5942-8
Ebook ISBN: 978-1-5107-5946-6

Photography: Pierre Javelle
Styling: Orathay Souksisavanh
Shopping: Christine Legeret
Designer: Sophie Villette
Editor: Anne Bazaugour
Proofreader: Véronique Dussidour

Cover design: Trisha Garner © Murdoch Books 2019

Publisher: Corinne Roberts
Translator: Melissa McMahon
English-language editor: Justine Harding
English-language designer: Susanne Geppert

Printed in China